Date Due

B C 4 Mar 84		
JUIN 23		
DEC 22		
JAN 5		
MAY 13		
DEC 28 2004		
APR 4		
JUN 1 5 2005		

203 p.   (Literature and life series)
Bibliography: p. 195-198.

1. Richler, Mordecai, 1931-   - Criticism
and interpretation.   I. Title.
08 0442l404   l715534 LC

V +lcon   6/He

MORDECAI RICHLER

Arnold E. Davidson

FREDERICK UNGAR PUBLISHING CO.
NEW YORK

Library of Congress Cataloging in Publication Data

Davidson, Arnold E., 1936–
    Mordecai Richler.

        (Literature and life series)
        Bibliography: p.
        Includes index.
        1. Richler, Mordecai, 1931–   —Criticism and
interpretation.   I. Title.   II. Series.
PR9199.3.R5Z63   1982   813'.54   82-40282
ISBN 0-8044-2140-4

Acknowledgments

I here again thank my wife, Dr. Cathy N. Davidson, for her long-sustained assistance during the writing of this book. I would also like to thank my typist, Dr. Donald Lewsader, for doing a superlative job in a very short time. A summer research grant from the Elmhurst College Alumni Association and a year's sabbatical leave from Elmhurst College to work on this project were both most appreciated. I am also grateful to the Michigan State University Library, for making its extensive Canadian holdings available to me while I was on sabbatical leave, and to both the University of Windsor Library and the University of British Columbia Library, for assistance rendered during visits to those campuses. Finally, I am particularly indebted to the staff at Elmhurst College Library for the help I have received while working on this and other projects.

Contents

Chronology

1967   Wins Canada Council senior arts fellowship.

1968   *Cocksure* and *Hunting Tigers under Glass: Essays and Reports* are published.

1968–69 Writer in residence at Sir George Williams University.

1969   *The Street* is published; receives Canadian Governor-General's award for *Cocksure.*

1970   Edits *Canadian Writing Today* anthology for Penguin and Peter Smith publishers.

1971   *St. Urbain's Horseman* is published.

1972   *Shovelling Trouble* is published; receives Canadian Governor-General's award for *St. Urbain's Horseman*; returns to Canada; becomes a member of the editorial board of the Book-of-the-Month Club.

1972–74 Visiting professor at Carleton University, Ottawa.

1974   *Notes on an Endangered Species* is published; authors screenplay of *The Apprenticeship of Duddy Kravitz*, which wins the Screenwriters Guild of America award for the best comedy and is nominated for an Academy Award.

1975   *Jacob Two-Two Meets the Hooded Fang* is published.

1976   *Jacob Two-Two* wins Canadian Bookseller's award for best children's book.

1977   Writes the text for *Images of Spain,* a book of photographs; coauthors screenplay *Fun with Dick and Jane.*

1978   *Great Comic Book Heroes and Other Essays* is published.

1980   *Joshua Then and Now* is published.

1

~.~.~.~.~.~.~.~.~.~.~.~.~.~.~.~.~.

The Street and Beyond: Starting Out in the Montreal Ghetto

Mordecai Richler begins his lightly fictionalized memoir *The Street* with two contrasting recollections. The first tells of starting out, the beginning of it all:

> One St. Urbain Street day cribs and diapers were cruelly withdrawn and the next we were scrubbed and carted off to kindergarten. Though we didn't know it, we were already in pre-med school. School starting age was six, but fiercely competitive mothers would drag protesting four-year-olds to the registration desk and say, "He's short for his age."
> "Birth certificate, please?"
> "Lost in a fire."
> On St. Urbain Street, a head start was all.

The other is an account of a recent event, his visit in 1967 to Montreal, the city he first left sixteen years earlier, and his immediate observation of how much (perhaps because of all those head starts) it had flourished:

Coming from dowdy London, via decaying New York, I was instantly struck by the city's affluence. As our jet dipped toward Dorval, I saw what appeared to be an endless glitter of eccentrically shaped green ink wells.

Suburban swimming pools. For Arty and Stan, Zelda, Pinky's Squealer, Nate, Fanny, Shloime, and Mrs. Klinger's rank-one boy; all the urchins who had learnt to do the dead man's float with me in the winding muddy Shawbridge river, condemned by the health board each August as a polio threat.

Much has been gained; much has been lost. "Place Ville Marie. The metro. Expo. Ile Notre Dame. Habitat. Place des Arts. This cornucopia certainly wasn't the city I had grown up in and quit."

Impressed by Expo and the vitality of Montreal, Richler decided to return again to serve for a year as writer-in-residence at his old school, Sir George Williams University. So he and his family were, as he puts it, back in Canada in 1968, "not so much new as retreaded Canadians." And again he was struck by change: "To come home in 1968 was to discover that it wasn't where I had left it—it had been bulldozed away—or had become, as is the case with St. Urbain, a Greek preserve." Faced with that fact, a writer of Richler's ability has only one choice. Words will put back what time and progress have taken away. In *The Street*, Richler recreates the world in which he grew up. Peopling that world, he puts in characters from his past—and from his fiction: a young Duddy Kravitz wheels and deals here very much as he does in the novel that partly takes his name. The artist also gives us a cagily indefinite rendering of himself. Most of the specifics of the memoir are consistent with Richler's own experience, but they are also consistent with that experience as it is refracted through earlier and later fictions. Or, in simpler terms, the narrator of *The Street* could be the young Mordecai Richler, but he could also be a younger version of Noah Adler in *Son of a Smaller Hero* or Jacob Hersh in *St. Urbain's Horseman.*

Richler? Or Adler? Or Hersh? To draw any such distinctions is perhaps arbitrary and unnecessary. Neither is the strict biographical accuracy of *The Street* an issue.[1] Richler would probably argue that the real life of an imaginative writer is the life that he imagines it to be. He would also certainly maintain—indeed, he has often done so—that the full details of the writer's real life are none of the critic's or the reader's business. Nor does he give, in *The Street,* full details for even the fictionalized protagonist's early years. The picture provided is a very generalized one. We see various childhood exploits. One episode tells how a few young boys visit a nearby summer resort, steal a sign that proclaims "THIS BEACH IS RESTRICTED TO GENTILES," alter it, and then plant on their own beach that sign, which now announces "THIS BEACH IS RESTRICTED TO LITVAKS." This account, incidentally, is taken directly from *Son of a Smaller Hero.* Another episode, perhaps more personal, gives an effective child's-eye view of a grandmother's protracted dying and the family tensions, obvious to the child but only half understood, that swirl around that event. We also see the adolescent boy groping toward the facts of life. One chapter, for example, details his fumbling attempts to put into practice the dubious expertise garnished from a study manual, *The Art of Kissing*, sold to him by the ever-enterprising Duddy Kravitz. But mostly *The Street* describes how the main character and his friends hung out on the street, grew up on the street, and, at the end of the work, were in process of leaving St. Urbain Street.

Some important facts of Richler's life still come through. He gives a thumbnail sketch of his own family history in the disconnected background information that fills out *The Street*. At one point he describes one grandfather who, "like so many others, ventured to Canada by steerage from a Gallician *shtetl*, in 1904, following hard on the outbreak of the Russo-Japanese War" and the pogroms that, in Poland and Russia, accompanied the war. He also tells of the unlikely accident whereby that grandfather ended up in Montreal and not Chicago, the city to which he was originally ticketed. Another man on the same ship had a train ticket to Montreal but had family in Chicago. The grandfather "knew somebody's cousin in Toronto" and knew that Toronto, like Montreal, was in Canada. The two men simply traded tickets, and then the one, arriving in Montreal, did not travel on to Toronto but settled in what was fast becoming the Montreal ghetto. The grandfather became a peddler. The father operated a junkyard. The son was originally intended to be a rabbi and then, after an early adolescent break with orthodox religion, a doctor. The three generations of this one family epitomize the essential immigrant saga that all around them was acted out in all of its small stages:

Slowly, unfalteringly, the immigrants began to struggle up a ladder of streets, from one where you had to leave your garbage outside your front door to another where you actually had a rear lane as well as a back yard where corn and tomatoes were usually grown; from the three rooms over the fruit store or tailor shop to your own cold-water flat. A street with trees.

The other grandfather, we learn elsewhere, was a rabbi. The mother's father "had been a Zaddik [a man of holiness and wisdom], . . . and I've been assured that to study Talmud with him had been an illuminating experience." He had also been, on his own terms, a successful writer: "My grandfather had written many books: a translation of the Book of Splendour (the Zohar) into modern Hebrew, some twenty years work, and lots of slender volumes of sermons, hasidic tales, and rabbinical commentaries. His books had been published in Warsaw and later in New York." This grandfather died when the grandson was a small child. Still, his literary accomplishment may have predisposed or encouraged his grandson to become a writer too. One son of Rabbi Judah Rosenberg did become a playwright; one daughter, at age seventy-five, published her own autobiography; the grandson, Mordecai Richler, is one of Canada's best writers and a major contemporary novelist.

A quite different crucial effect of the maternal grandfather is also evident. The characters most fully developed in *The Street* are the protagonist's parents. What most characterizes them is the obviously unhappy marriage that they, for the most part separately, endure. The nature of that unhappiness is carefully analyzed.

It is an unhappiness in which the maternal grandfather plays a significant role. The mother, enamored with the noble qualities of her own father, deeply believes that she has married beneath herself. The husband's passive acquiescence to his wife's disapproval further demonstrates, so far as she is concerned, how unworthy he is. The circle spins sadly on in *The Street* and spins also in different Richler plots. The fictional protagonists—from Noah Adler in *Son of a Smaller Hero* to Joshua Shapiro in *Joshua Then and Now*—who emerge from the Montreal ghetto also come out of the same flawed family, the same family that produced the author. And that conclusion does not derive from the different testimonies of the author alone. The mother has recently published her autobiography, a work that demonstrates "how thoroughly Richler has plundered his own life for material to use in his novels." The same review of Leah Rosenberg's *The Errand Runner: Reflections of a Rabbi's Daughter* continues:

Mrs. Rosenberg's sporadic account offers documentary evidence to support the true identity of her literary counterparts. Leah Adler in *Son of a Smaller Hero*, Maw in [the] collection of autobiographical short stories *The Street*, and Mrs. Hersh in *St. Urbain's Horseman* are all heavies; all worship their god-like fathers, and either were or are desperately unhappy in their marriages; all are virtually indistinguishable from the woman we meet in *The Errand Runner*.[2]

There are two other points raised in *The Street* that must be briefly discussed. First, the book is a memoir of a certain place *and time*. The place is Montreal and more specifically the ghetto of Montreal. The time is the forties and more specifically the early forties and the years of World War II. The war is marked in various ways; by, for example, an influx of refugees. Those refugees, "mostly German and Austrian Jews," recapitulate the history of the more eastern European Jews who fled the pogroms of the early twentieth century. They also call to mind the Jews who were not lucky enough to escape from Europe. "For our grandparents who remembered those left behind in Rumania and Poland the war was a time of unspeakable grief." For the grandchildren, however, it was a time for playing at war games, for buying "on the black market" the American comic books that had been "banned for the duration." That childhood unconcern has long haunted Richler, the mature writer. Old enough to understand what was happening but too young to participate, he necessarily missed the second crucial test (the first, for Richler, was the Spanish Civil War) of the century. As Sandra Martin observes:

This sense of alienation, of never being part of the action, of always being out of step with people and events, is a principal theme in his work. . . . In each of his serious novels Richler has [also] drawn a battered survivor of the war, a living if wounded symbol of what it meant to commit oneself to The Cause.[3]

The dichotomy here, however, is not just the contrast between young boys playing at war and young men dying in earnest. It runs much deeper. "For my generation the war was hearing of death and sacrifice but seeing with our own eyes the departure from cold-water flats to apartments in Outremont, duplexes and split-levels in the suburbs." The "uprising in the Warsaw ghetto" could take place concomitantly with "the changeover," in Montreal, "from poky little *shuls* to big synagogue-cum-parochial schools with stained glass windows and mosaics outside." In short, while the Jews of the Old World were being murdered by millions, the Jews of the New World "never had it so good." That opposition gives rise to monstrous questions of monstrous injustice and partly explains why Richler as a writer can be both the sternest of moralists and the most savage of satirists. He himself has observed that "I write out of a kind of disgust with things as they are,"[4] and, even more to the point, "what I am looking for are the values with which in this time a man can live with honour."[5]

The war emphasizes the fact of this author's Jewish heritage. As the narrator of *The Street* insists: "Our world, its prizes and punishments, was entirely Jewish." Yet *The Street* also shows how this entirely Jewish world is contained in a larger world that is inescapably Canadian. So the second point to be noted is Richler's divided heritage as a Jewish Canadian writer, a Jewish Canadian writer who grew up in the city that is the focus of still a different division in Canada itself, the split between English Canada and French Canada. The French Canadians, Richler observes in *The Street*, "although our enemies were not entirely unloved. Like us, they were poor and coarse with large families and spoke English badly." They, too, were subject to demeaning stereotypes and various petty and not-so-petty persecutions. "It was only the WASPs who were truly hated and feared. 'Among them,' I heard it said, 'with those porridge faces, who can tell what they're thinking?' It was, we felt, their country, and given sufficient liquor who knew when they would make trouble?" In a ghetto within a ghetto, discriminations received reflected back as discriminations inflicted. "Pea-soups [French Canadians] were for turning the lights on and off on the sabbath and running elevators and cleaning out chimneys and furnaces. . . . The French Canadians were our *schwartzes* [Yiddish for 'blacks']." And again the war emphasizes divisions, oppositions. "I can recall seeing swastikas and *'A bas les Juifs'* ['Down with the Jews'] painted on the Laurentian highway." There were restricted hotels and country clubs, university quotas, racial incidents in the street. "The democracy we were being invited to defend was flawed and hostile to us. Without question it was better for us in Canada than in Europe, but this was still their country, not ours."

The young boy still in Montreal can make that statement. The older Richler, already entered into what long seemed as if it might be a permanent exile, knew better. In one of his first interviews after achieving some success as a writer in exile, he observed, "I am not a European writer and I couldn't become one if I stayed here twenty-five years. All my attitudes are Canadian; I'm a Canadian; there's nothing to be done about it."[6] The statement, made in London in 1956, was an accurate self-assessment. Except for a few interruptions, the London exile continued for another sixteen years, until Richler's permanent return to Canada in 1972. During that time Richler, as a writer, remained resolutely Canadian. All of his major characters are Canadian, sometimes Canadians in exile. All, except the first, are viewed through a broad perspective and portrayed with a balance and control largely fostered by Richler's own divided Canadian heritage. As one major critic has observed, "Canada is a land of minorities, regions, disguised ghettoes. In that lies Richler's appeal to his countrymen, and the reason why, twenty years away from Montreal, he is never considered as other than a Canadian writer."[7] Or, as a different critic puts the same matter: "His ambivalence, his irony, his ability to hold a number of perspectives and attitudes in tension—these are Canadian."[8] The representative function of Richler's nationality is perfectly summed up by another major Canadian novelist who observes that just as "it is important . . . to *be* black in Zimbabwe in a time of revolution," so is it important "to *be* Canadian in a time of cultural crisis."[9]

"To be a Jew and a Canadian" should be, then, a double plus. In a sense it is. To be both, Richler maintains, "is to emerge from the ghetto twice."[10] To emerge is to achieve some perspective. And Richler's emerged protagonists tell, as they regularly do, their own story. They can celebrate, in that story, how far they have come, how much they have liberated themselves from the circumstances of their birth. But to celebrate the escape is also to look back at the cage escaped from and, sometimes, to see it more clearly. "The ghetto of Montreal," Richler writes in his second novel, "has no real walls and no true dimensions. The walls are the habit of atavism and the dimensions are an illusion. But the ghetto exists all the same." That complex recognition is of a different order from the celebrating exclamation: "Free at last! Thank God, I'm free at last!" One perspective leads to another. The early claim, "How far I have come!" becomes a nagging question, "Have I come far at all?" This complex interplay of situation and perspective and a grappling with not the flattering first assertion but the denigrating second question gives Richler's serious fiction its characteristic tone. It is a characteristically Canadian tone of "criticizing, always, the things I believe in or I'm attached to."[11] In contrast, the typical American reaction is to assert the first apparent progress, "How far I have come!" and thereby validate some version of the American dream. Of course, as Richler continues, his "very perverse kind of love" is not always appreciated by its recipients. He does "appear to be very critical of Canada" and has "been accused of being an anti-Semite."[12] Yet that same perversely questioning love does make him a passionately concerned and powerfully convincing observer of the small world that he surveys.

Up to this point we have looked at mostly the early life of the writer, as it is somewhat fictionally presented in *The Street*, primarily to understand the ways in which that life helped to shape the fiction. The remainder of this introductory chapter will be a brief overview of the author's biography as it continues beyond the ending of *The Street*. In best *bildungsroman* fashion, the young protagonist of that work had progressed, by the end of the book, from the province—i.e., the ghetto—to a minor center of civilization and culture. He had done so without traveling very far. Still in Montreal, he enrolled in Sir George Williams College because his grades were not good enough to get him into McGill, one of Canada's premier universities and also located in Montreal. What came next? The answer is appropriately romantic: Paris, the greatest of all French cities. After two years as an English major at Sir George Williams, Richler decided that the academic treadmill was not for him. "I became frightened that if I got a B.A. I'd get an M.A. and then I might try for a Ph.D., and that would be the end."[13] He withdrew from school, cashed in an insurance policy into which his mother had paid fifty cents a week for years, and departed for Europe.

Richler left Canada in 1951 to escape the provincialism of the fifties and to pursue more seriously his still nascent career as an author. He had begun writing when he "was about fourteen . . . foolish things in a very haphazard way."[14] This was about the same time that he broke from his formal religious training and ceased to attend

Jewish parochial school. At Baron Byng High School (represented as Fletcher's Field High School in several of his works) he did not distinguish himself but apparently enjoyed a few English courses and attempted to duplicate some of the romantic stories in one of his high school anthologies. Even in college, however, he was still wavering between art and literature. He had "facility" with art, had done some work with advertising firms during the two years he was a student at Sir George Williams, but concluded that he would be, at best, "a third-rate commercial artist."[15] It was at this point that he decided on Paris and literature. He went, however, not in the post–World War I Hemingway tradition, to discover life, art, and the city itself, and to create a new literature out of those experiences, but to find other like-minded young would-be writers who could assure him that his as yet untested commitment to writing and his flight from Canada made sense. He was successful in that search. "Yes, I found friends and social support for the first time in my life, and here were people who felt as I did, and who disliked many of the same things I did."[16] Those friends included a number of young American and Canadian writers who would also soon make a name for themselves: David Burnett, Mavis Gallant, Mason Hoffenberg, Terry Southern, David Stacton, Alexander Trochi, and others. And in Paris the "callow kid of nineteen," who did not originally intend to do so, of course discovered his true university. "St. Germain des Pres was my campus, Montparnasse my frat house, and my two years there are a sweetness I retain, as others do wistful memories of McGill or Oxford."[17]

In Paris Richler regularly turned out realistic short stories that, submitted to such major American magazines as *Esquire* and *Harper's*, were just as regularly returned. Then, during a brief visit to Spain, he wrote in six weeks an apprentice novel. He revised it, discarded it, and then wrote another. A friend persuaded Richler to submit this novel, *The Acrobats*, for possible publication, which he did shortly before he left Paris to return to Canada. Back in Canada after two years in Europe, Richler worked at various jobs and then found a more regular position with the Canadian Broadcasting Corporation. All the while he was revising *The Acrobats* according to suggestions made by both the agent who had first read the manuscript and the editor of a possible publishing company. The novel, however, was soon sold to still another publisher who also had still other suggestions for revision. Finally, in 1954, the first novel was published, and Richler again left Canada, this time for England, now even more determined to support himself by his writings. He also left Canada in order to work in a larger arena than Canada allowed. Success in his own country, he feared, might come too easily. "It's dangerous because it is out of proportion."[18] With a characteristic concern for perspective, he wanted to test his "sense of his own worth" against the publishing standards of London and New York, not just against those of Toronto.

That test has been conclusively passed.

While living in London Richler completed his next six novels. These works would be published in England, and generally in America too, before they appeared in Canada. As a consequence, they were often better received in England and the United States than in Canada. But more and more the books demonstrated the promise that the *Times Literary Supplement* saw in the first of Richler's written-in-London novels. As the anonymous early reviewer asserted, "there can be no doubt of his [Richler's] prodigal talent."[19] Richler, out of economic necessity, also became a successful writer in other mediums. He has worked as author or collaborator (movie writing, he complains, is done by committee) on several screenplays including *Room at the Top, Life at the Top, The Looking Glass War,* and *Fun with Dick and Jane.* He also adapted from his own novel *The Apprenticeship of Duddy Kravitz* the script for the movie of the same title, a script that won two awards and was nominated for an Academy Award. In still another medium, Richler has written a voluminous quantity of journalism and reviews for major British, American, and Canadian magazines. He is the author of one children's book, *Jacob Two-Two Meets the Hooded Fang*; one travel book, *Images of Spain*; a drama, *The Bells of Hell;* and some ten or so radio and television plays. He has edited, too, the Penguin anthology, *Canadian Writing Today,* and since 1972 has served as a judge for the Book-of-the-Month Club. He has been, in short, for almost thirty years a "complete writer" in the eighteenth-century fashion and shows, as much as any contemporary author, that even in these fallen (from the serious writer's point of view) times one can live professionally by and for the written word without selling out.[20]

Richler's productivity has, however, its obverse side. Much material is recycled and then sometimes recycled again. As a professional writer, and Richler is a very professional writer, little is wasted. For example, a short story, "Mortimer Griffin, Shalinsky, and How They Settled the Jewish Question," was published first in *Tamarack Review* in 1958; a considerably longer reworked version was next published in *Maclean's* in 1961; and, reworked once more, the story finally grew into the novel *Cocksure*. Or an essay, "This Year in Jerusalem," was written originally for a national magazine, was revised to be reprinted in one collection of essays, was reprinted in still another essay collection, and was then partly incorporated in still a different form into *St. Urbain's Horseman*. A number of the essays such as "Why I Write" and "Writing for the Movies" are printed in three of the four separate collections of essays, while the essays themselves are sometimes composites of shorter pieces and reviews. Because of such reworking and reprinting, Richler is sometimes charged with a deficiency of imagination. Yet the very extent of his work substantially counters that charge. Furthermore, by financially utilizing to the fullest his journalistic writing (which is where most of the "recycling" takes place), Richler avoids the need either to popularize or to rush his novels. The writing that pays allows time for the writing that counts, and, as a novelist, Richler admits that he is "increasingly critical" of his fiction, that he works more and more slowly.[21] So it is hardly fair to criticize the expedients that support his habit and habits (revising extensively) as a serious novelist.

"The public part of my life is my books. The rest is not very important."[22] Richler, on principle, is intensely private about the rest. "Whether a writer is a marvelously charming, agreeable, generous man or whether he beats his wife and tortures his children is beside the point. . . . The books are what matter one way or another and the two should not be confused."[23] This self-protective philosophy is made all the more defensible by Richler's telling assessment of one most obvious contrary example. His essay "Norman Mailer" is a devastating picture of the travesty that ensues when a talented writer trades on his personality more than on his work. Nevertheless, one significant event in the private life of this public writer must be finally considered, and that is his so-far-permanent return to Canada in 1972.

Richler himself has connected his return with his writing. "Certainly the primary reason why I'm back is that I feel I've somehow lost a sense of continuity. . . . And so I've come back here in search of some kind of renewal."[24] Putting the same matter still more succinctly, he found it necessary to return to what he termed "the roots of my discontent."[25] There is something quintessentially Canadian in that return to Canada. As numerous commentators have noted, an important theme in Canadian literature stands in definite opposition to the Thomas Wolfe dicta that you can't go home again. Such major Canadian writers as Margaret Atwood, Robertson Davies, Margaret Laurence, and Richler himself show again and again that not only can you go home again, you also must. The flight for identity, in the Canadian mythos, requires at least an imaginative return to the past fled from. Examples of this mythos in action include Atwood's *Surfacing*, Davies's Deptford trilogy, Laurence's *The Diviners*, and certainly Richler's *St. Urbain's Horseman* and *Joshua Then and Now* as well as the earlier *Son of a Smaller Hero*. But especially in Richler's two most recent novels, the past that would be abandoned is a deadening weight until it is rediscovered or even reinvented and thereby reincorporated into the protagonist's psyche. Canadian authors apparently fare no better in these matters than do Canadian protagonists. Like other expatriates—Robert Kroetsch, Margaret Laurence, Gabrielle Roy—Richler went home again, but to a different home. He fled two ghettos when he left Canada. He recreated both ghettos time and time again in his subsequent fiction. He goes home to his own reinvented lost world as well as to his considerably altered country. As his most recent novel, *Joshua Then and Now* (written back in Canada), demonstrates, his art has not suffered because of his return.

Yet Richler himself provides another perspective on this biographical capstone to his career so far. Writing, he once observed, is a "cottage industry."[26] Can it matter that much, then, where the cottage is located? And even more disconcerting for the biographically minded critic, does what goes on within the cottage, other than the writing, matter either? Richler insists that it does not. "I fervently believe that all a writer should send into the marketplace to be judged is his own work; the rest should remain private."[27] The rest of this study will be consistent with that pronouncement and will be restricted to an assessment of the main body of work whereby Richler wishes to be judged, the eight novels he has written so far, starting with the first.

2

~.~.~.~.~.~.~.~.~.~.~.~.~.~.~.~.~.~.

The Acrobats:
A First Try at
Artistic Balance

It would be an act of charity to pass rather briefly over *The Acrobats*. Some first novels such as Ernest Hemingway's *The Sun Also Rises* announce, as with the sound of trumpets, the arrival of a new and major talent. Others—William Faulkner's *Soldier' Pay* or Saul Bellow's *Dangling Man* come immediately to mind—show the author still struggling to find a subject and a voice. They merit our attention mostly as intimations of better things to come. Mordecai Richler's first novel can definitely be placed in that second category. In this ironically titled work (an irony surely unintended) the young novelist—Richler was only twenty-three when the book was published—regularly misses the artistic balance that he tries to strike. Realistic and symbolic details are frequently confused. Plot and character keep getting out of hand, or, more accurately, characters are required to act out of character by the unlikely demands of the strained plot. The often inflated language serves only to emphasize that the writer has not achieved the effects for which he too obviously struggles. Such mistakes do not recur in the later fiction, but they loom large in this first story of a confused young man searching for himself in post-war Spain.

An inconsistency in details frequently blurs the issues—whatever they are, for they are often unclear—set forth in *The Acrobats*. Consider, to take just one example, the numerous scenes suggesting the symbolic rats gnawing at the detritus of the wasteland world portrayed in this novel. Considerable attention is also paid to the literal rats that infest the protagonist's seedy artist apartment, rats that he walls away from his bed with a barricade of books and bottles and painting equipment. That protection, possible proof against the symbolic rat, would not of course keep the literal one at bay. Furthermore, when André Bennett, the protagonist, temporarily subsides into a long incipient madness, the first symptom of his insanity is the delusion, clearly shown to be a delusion, that a rat is crawling up his body. Is the reader then being pelted with literal or symbolic rats? If symbolic, what do they signify? As the following quote amply illustrates, Richler often goes to considerable length to magnify the significance of his rodents, and to deflate them too:

Listening to the darkness, he was conscious of the sharp scuffle of the rats and the loud beating of his heart. Puffing flaccidly at his cigarette, his last link with sanity, he tried to shake from his mind the persistent visual image of a decapitated dead rat. Inky spurts of blood trickled slowly out of the rat's neck. The grey body coughed convulsively and the belly gradually flattened out like a punctured tube. He watched the lighted end of his cigarette butt shudder in the darkness. There was no longer an outer objective world. (And perhaps, he thought with sudden delirious vision, there never was.)

Finally, and with many misgivings, he switched on the light. A rat scurried across the bedroom floor . . .

A more fundamental flaw is a persistent confusion of character. We are clearly meant to take the protagonist seriously, to mourn his death. André Bennett is greatly admired—for no obvious reason, it should be added—by almost all those who come in contact with him. After his untimely demise we also hear a whole series of testimonies on what a great artist he would have been if only . . . Yet the novel also shows that he is a seriously disturbed young man who is often drunk, always inept, and who finally simply throws his life away. Twice, for example, he is provided with the money he claimed he needed to escape from Spain with Toni, the girl whom he believes he loves. Once he loses the necessary cash when he unthinkingly turns his pockets inside out to show a persistent beggar that he has nothing to give, and—oops—a hundred dollar bill falls into the medicant's hands. Later, another friend also gives André a substantial sum, specifically designating that with this cash he is to save Toni by taking her away. But soon afterwards, out in the street, André allows himself to be picked up by a prostitute and then, in her room, pays her everything he has with him for the services that he neither wants nor receives. Equally dubiously, when he finally concludes that he will marry Toni and that they will "somehow" go back to Canada and be happy, he concomitantly decides that he will not fight Colonel Kraus, the elderly ex-Olympic athlete and ex-Nazi who is his rival for Toni's favors and a man André had earlier said he would kill. Naturally, he immediately encounters Kraus, persists in the subsequent fight, and gets himself killed, despite the fact that, as we are later explicitly told, Kraus at first had no intention of doing anything more than "teaching him a lesson" by winning the fight.

The "psychological" explanation of that climactic encounter provided in the novel only compounds the problem of inconsistency. Unknown to André, Toni is pregnant. Another man had "forced himself" on her before she met André, whom she immediately loves "with a hopeless beautiful love," despite the awkward fact of the pregnancy and her suspicions that her passion can never be returned. We see her desperate to win his love, determined to help him past the crisis of conscience (more of which later) that keeps him from loving, and dreaming of their possible future together. So it makes no sense at all when she subsequently decides to solace the rejected "suitor." Out of pure sympathy for his disappointment (and that is the motive given in the text—"You must try to understand, André. He was crying like a child. I felt sorry for him."), she admits her former persecutor (and that is how he is portrayed in the text) to her bed. This unlikely charity identifies for André his rival. Indeed, he almost catches the two of them *in flagrante delicto*. The other man, of course, is Colonel Kraus. André, without any special provocation, had already threatened to kill that gentleman. Now he has real reason to try to do so and soon makes the attempt, even though we are also told that he overcomes his hatred of Kraus.

This episode of infidelity is contrived in another way. It serves to show the reader that, of the two, André, despite his inability to love, really was the more faithful lover. With the prostitute, with an older woman, Jessie Larkin, who once picked him up—strange that he should be so easily picked up—the act was never consummated. But his near falls are canceled out when, confronting an undressed Toni and an unmade bed, he immediately rises to the occasion. "I understand," he lied. "I love you and I understand." He also goes on to deliver the proposal that, at the request of a friend and not prompted by his own desires, he had come to make. Presently, he does understand. He then wants, from his own heart and not because of his promise to Chaim (a substitute father to both André and Toni and the man who gave André the money to save her), to marry her. How sad that he is killed before he can tell her so—and how contrived.

It is hard to take the sorrows of these ill-starred lovers seriously for still another reason. They are not so much believable characters as literary clichés. To start with, Toni is perilously close to that ancient figure of male wish-fulfillment, the beautiful prostitute with a heart of gold waiting to be saved by the love of a good man. About her profession, there is a little waffling in the novel. She asserts that she is a dance-hall hostess, although others imply that she is something less. The distinction between selling dances and selling sex is, admittedly, sometimes hard to draw. But, about her heart of gold, there is no doubt, as her love for André and her kindness to Kraus equally attest. Futhermore, Richler apparently concurs in the generous assessment of Toni that the other characters regularly proclaim. Why else would he bring in, in a concluding and unnecessary "Afterwards," an intrusive character, an American academic in Paris, who suddenly appears on the scene for no other purpose than to marry Toni, to make her happy, and to support the illegitimate child she has born. The one sardonic touch that keeps all of this from being pure soap opera is the observation that the child is "beginning to look more and more like Kraus." And André too, searching for the values and vision that in a crass society will enable him to achieve his full potential, is very much the conventional portrait of the artist as a confused and misunderstood young man.

Other characters apparently intended to be novel examples of basic types also come across as standard, stock-in-trade figures. We encounter early Barney Larkin, a crass American businessman who prices everything and values nothing. His wife Jessie is the Margot Macomber model of American womanhood, still beautiful, bitchy, and even more determined with advancing middleage to manipulate and humiliate the husband who pays the bills. Chaim, the Jewish father figure previously mentioned, manages to combine the two roles of grandfatherly Jewish sage and wandering Jew. Colonel Kraus (the name is suspiciously close to Kraut) is almost mindless in his automatic recourse to brutality. His sister is the coldly rational fascist. She has a Ph.D. She also has a face that is "dry and tanned" and a body "thin, without sex, and the colour of old paper." Not surprisingly, she is a desperately lonely widow, too proud to admit her need for love, and ready to kill the man who spurns her indirect attentions. Or there is "crazy Jeem," a character only referred to in the book. This salt-of-the-earth, American black Republican soldier irrepressibly pinched attractive bottoms, made beautiful music (naturally) on his harmonica, and naively wondered "maybe if someone explained things to Franco, how the people really felt . . ." (ellipsis in the original).

The language too is often strained, stilted. Note, for example, how Pepe, another old freedom fighter, and his wife Maria discuss the death of "Jeem," killed during the Spanish Civil War:

"Why did he die, Maria? What did it mean?"

"I don't know."

"But you're religious. You believe these things happen for a reason." . . .

"Maybe he died for you?"

He found her solemn face in the dark. Her deep black eyes were without expression and her lovely lips were quiet.

"For me?"
"So that you might understand something."
"What?"
"I don't know."

The passage falters under the weight of tragic meaning that it is supposed to carry, and the tolling refrain "I don't know," along with the necessarily unspecific "something," only emphasizes how little has been said. But much of the novel is even more obviously overwritten. On the same page as the excerpt just quoted, we find a brief disconnected poetic setting of scene: "Moon of the type in demand by sentimental virgins, i.e., pretty as a postcard moon, harvest moon, moon like from a story in *Good Housekeeping*." On the next page we are made privy to André's musings of the moment:

If anyone had asked him the hour—yesterday, now, tomorrow—he would have replied, ineluctably: "Five Minutes to the End."
. . . five minutes to when the mob plunging madly down the metro steps would be called to a halt, forced to stare into each other's eyes; five minutes to when the bankers and the priests of liedom would feel the finger of God hot on their backs, the irrevocable what's what finally demanded . . . five minutes to when the squint-eyed clerks and the whores humpbacked by sin are told to bring their indifferent copulating to a stop . . . (ellipsis in the original)

But why go on even though the list continues for most of a page, with still more versions of the impending end.

The novel itself is the story of an anti-hero

for an empty time. The anti-hero is André Bennett, a young expatriate Canadian who aspires to be an artist but "could not paint, not really, so long as men were killing each other so often." The time is the very early fifties, shortly after the Second World War. The time is also Spain of the early fifties, and I say "time" not "place" because André is no standard tourist interested in seeing the sights of the country. Instead, searching for recent history, "he came to Spain, Valencia, where the killing had started in a way and [where] maybe they could explain it." More specifically, he hopes that, at the site of the first confrontation with fascism, he will come to understand how that confrontation led to a world at war and then, despite the fascists losing World War II, to the moral chaos of the time. It is a big "it" he wants explained, but his condition is desperate. Foreseeing "his doom inevitable," he sees himself as one who "belonged to the last generation of men," not the "lost" one. The lost generation had it easy—"all Gods dead, all wars fought, all faiths in men shaken." One is almost nostalgic for those good old days: "There was going to be another war all right," muses André in the present time of the novel. "The old Gods, newly cleaned and pressed, were being gleefully handed down by the generations that had made an orgy of self-destruction out of the twenties, and an abysmal flop out of the thirties, only to reap the bloody harvest of the forties."

He comes to Spain hoping that he will learn to understand "it," to live with "it." All he discovers is that "it" still goes on, and "it" kills.

Correlative to the chaos of recent history is the fallen state of his present world. Even as he engages in the reflections just described, the "stink of stale drainage and decaying fish clogged his nostrils"; he sees the "illuminated chalk slogans and obscenities" that deface "damp peeling walls" beneath which "discarded old men" sleep while "lice [go] creeping up their faces." Images of rot and corruption pervade the novel. They characterize the city ("The heat smelled of rancid food, children with soiled underwear, uncovered garbage, venereal diseases, sweat and boils"); its inhabitants ("sluts bargained here and there with fading gallants, and the aloof bourgeois in their mean black suits, sweating, unimpressed, just a bit too conscious of the stink of their bodies, idled about glumly, their pious wives dangling like dumplings from their sides"); its visitors ("Sweating, the tourists felt the gas and acids contained in their bellies . . . an awareness of small deaths, many of them, rotting their bodies bit by bit"); and even André's dreams ("Rats [rats again] floating in pools of gangrene had clogged the streets again"). In this respect the brief epigraph from Antonio Machado, translated in the text, sets the tone for the whole volume: "It was a time of lies, of infamy." The Spain of Machado's poem, "poor, squalid, and drunken," the Spain of the novel, sets forth an image of a world gone wrong, not a history of how it got that way nor, even less, a prescription for its cure.

André's past is at one with his present. The product of a fabulously rich family, he is also the evidence of the failure of riches. His parents were estranged from each other and from their son. The father made money; the mother had affairs. André was deemed the product of one of those affairs by his father, he tells Toni, because he was "unbalanced," i.e., "rebellious," and by his mother "because it all would have been so utterly romantic." From that dubious childhood he grows up to achieve disasters of his own. At university he takes up with an iconoclastic and somewhat neurotic "notorious" Jewish girl, Ida Blumberg. He plans a rebellious marriage "that would show everyone," but she becomes pregnant first and insists on an abortion. When, after the operation, he does not hear from her, he visits her parents to be told by the hysterically grieving father, "She is dead . . . . She died with your filth inside her." The consequences of the abortion, which include the unlikely act of the accused "murderer" hitting the "old and wizened" orthodox Mr. Blumberg and knocking him to the floor, are, of course, the source of André's debilitating guilt and the reason why it takes him so long to decide that he can love Toni. With Toni he has another chance to do right by a woman with a child, but, as has been noted, he fails again and fails perhaps because his continuing guilt cannot be assuaged by anything short of his own death.

The novel, however, is not just the story of André. As George Bowering has pointed out, "We watch not the performance of one man's life, but the tumbling pattern of the human condition. Each player hides his own version of guilt, secret from the rest. The recent past in each case haunts the present, and promises no good future—for any of the characters of the novel, for Spain, for [the] mid-century World."[1] We see the human pattern in miniature in several different ways. Some of the subsidiary characters embody different versions of the same themes that are basic to André and his story. Barney Larkin, the successful American businessman, and his faithless wife Jessie are a reduced version of André's unhappy parents. Barney Larkin, né Lazarus and married to Jessie Raymond "of the Jacksonville Raymonds," also corresponds to Ida Blumberg revolting against her past and to numerous other characters cut off, intentionally or otherwise, from their own heritage. Still other characters reflect the political condition of the time. Colonel Kraus, for example, recapitulates in his private life the history of fascism in twentieth-century Europe. He also, significantly, is alive and flourishing at the end of the novel. Kraus and his sister, however, also sound one of the more strained dark notes in the novel. Their love-hate relationship culminates with her suicide by hanging and him, on finding her dead, both "ripp[ing] open her blouse" to expose her breasts and "punch[ing] her solidly in the stomach." With Kraus's incestuous rage at the woman who hitherto has run his life, as with the explanation of André's guilt, a certain amount of not completely digested Freud grumbles noticeably from the bowels of the novel.[2]

As significant as any of the other background characters are the *fallas*, the huge wooden and papier-mâché caricature figures that are part of the festival at Valencia. These figures first preside over the festivities; then, stuffed with fireworks, they are burned on the last night of the celebration. They are, in short, T. S. Eliot's "Hollow Men" writ large, silently waiting for an end that will be marked, in their case, not with a whimper but a bang—a considerable bang. The sound and fury of their burning signifies that the festival is over and presages the nothing to follow. It is no accident that André's death occurs concomitantly with the minor apocalypse of the flaming and exploding *fallas.* The *fallas,* of course, are also traditional scapegoat figures. Yet the novel questions the efficacy of the scapegoat by providing an explicit (perhaps a too explicit) account of the whole scapegoat process: "Perhaps in all of us there is some evil and we're just too weak to burn it. So we build evil toys and dance around them, later we burn them. Hoping, perhaps, that it will help."

A novel describing various lost characters in search of themselves in Spain, while all around them a thematically significant festival unfolds, must call to mind Hemingway's *The Sun Also Rises.* The few ineffectual anarchist, communist, and socialist revolutionaries in *The Acrobats,* who solace themselves by looking back to the glorious but failed campaign against fascism, provide also a sad postscript to *For Whom the Bell Tolls.* The Hemingway connection is obvious in other ways. Much of the dialogue is in this major American author's characteristic spare style. Furthermore, some of Richler's phrasings are lifted almost directly from the earlier writer. André, for example, at one point proclaims how words "like *courage, soul, beautiful, honor*" and others, especially "love," have become "almost obscene." In similar fashion, Frederic Henry in *A Farewell to Arms* reads much those same words out of the English language. But not too much should be made of the influence of Hemingway. In clear contradistinction to Hemingway's first Spanish novel, Richler (as Bowering suggests) portrays a Spain in which the sun mostly sets. Unlike Hemingway's morally and politically engaged second Spanish novel, which clearly affirmed its "No man is an island" epigraph, Richler shows practically every man to be an island and a sinking one at that.

The Acrobats is a badly flawed novel. Overly contrived and often derivative, it too facilely expresses a "fashionably fifties" angst that lacks the courage of its own convictions. The novel is "irrevocably dated."[3] Certainly, *The Sun Also Rises* from the twenties speaks more immediately to the contemporary reader than does *The Acrobats* from the fifties. Yet the latter work can still elicit interest. As the critic just quoted also observes: "The relationships between the figures in the novel—major and minor— are worked out in an elaborate pattern in which nothing is gratuitous, everything linked by act or mental association."[4] Richler, even in this first novel, shows a concern for structure. We also see an intelligence alert to the shortcomings of the time as well as a sharp eye that will serve him more effectively in the later fiction and particularly in the explicit social satires, *The Incomparable Atuk* and *Cocksure*. Also, although the symbolic details sometimes strain toward statement—the rats squeaking under the significance they are required to bear—they also sometimes work surprisingly well—the *fallas*, for example. But most of all, as George Woodcock, a major Canadian critic, has observed, we see the first working of what will become "constant Richler themes— . . . the difficulties of communication between individuals, races, sexes, generations, traditions," and in that latter case the difficulties that are especially seen in the uneasy dealings between Jews and gentiles.[5]

To that short list one additional item should be added. Despite its exaggerated "excremental" vision, *The Acrobats* also evinces a generous humanity on the part of the young author that expresses itself most clearly through a sympathy for those usually considered beyond the pale of human consideration.[6] Chaim, the old Jew, can understand how desperate and lonely Frau Kraus is and how it must pain her to have to ask him, even indirectly, for help. Colonel Kraus at one point can pose a moral question to himself: "What if the things I did were wrong, what if the dead really weren't bad?" Crude Barney Larkin can defend himself from the mocking superiority of his brother-in-law: "Why do you always treat me as if I was a jerk? You guys who went to Spain and all that were supposed to be interested in your fellow men. Well, waddiya think I am?'' It is a defense that will later inform much of one of Richler's best novels, *The Apprenticeship of Duddy Kravitz*. In short, in *The Acrobats* we see the apprentice artist taking his faltering first steps. But they are first steps.

3

Son of a Smaller Hero:
The Protagonist Claims His Majority

If The Acrobats *partly represents* Richler's youthful tribute to Hemingway, *Son of a Smaller Hero* pays homage to F. Scott Fitzgerald. Gone is the staged, laconic Hemingwayesque language, the Spanish setting replete with hints of death in the afternoon, the quasi-existential test of the protagonist's manhood. Richler now resorts to occasionally baroque expository passages, to descriptions of mundane, realistic settings that are still, somehow, portentously symbolic, to the careful placing of events that both romanticize and undermine the story of a protagonist's initiation into adulthood. Essentially, *Son of a Smaller Hero* is an episode of love in the life of a young man searching for values. The hero, Noah Adler, combines the dreamy desiring of Jay Gatsby, the ironic detachment of Nick Carraway (the narrator of *The Great Gatsby*), and the nostalgic and necessarily futile attempts to elude and to recapture the past that must be attributed to Fitzgerald himself.

Yet *Son of a Smaller Hero* also sets forth another portrait of a would-be artist as a young man. As such it can be seen—so another critic has observed—as Richler's second "first novel." The work, George Woodcock observes, presents "somewhat realistically the problems, aspirations and agonies of a young writer" and thus serves as a kind of "initiation rite" preparatory to the more mature work to follow.[1] The young artist is present in another way too. Despite the author's prefatory disclaimer that the novel is "a novel not a biography,"we are tempted to draw parallels between the writer and his protagonist. In both cases we have a young man striving to escape the ghetto of Montreal, the provincialism of Canada, and the rawness of his own inexperience. Furthermore, Noah Adler, the sometimes flawed and often callow young hero who is the subject of the novel, is portrayed with a kind of forgiving indulgence that suggests at least sublimated autobiography. In subsequent books Richler was not again so tender-minded.

There is still another way in which *Son of a Smaller Hero* is an apprentice work. It is one of Richler's most simply narrated novels. A basically realistic story is presented by an objective narrator who can resort to omniscience whenever extra information seems appropriate. Thus the reader is regularly provided with summary background information that serves to elucidate the actions of both the major and the subsidiary characters in the plot. Both Miriam Hall, Noah's married mistress, and Theo Hall, the deceived husband, for example, are explained in terms of a strained relationship to the parent of the opposite sex. The narrator, always privy to Noah's thoughts, can also tell us what any of the other

characters are thinking. One scene is nothing
more than the contrasted musings of eight separate characters. The novel is also kept simple
by a straightforward chronological narration.
The action runs from chapter one, "Summer 1952," to chapter five, "Autumn and Winter
1953–54." Each chapter gives us the time of the
action described. Those times fit together more
to emphasize the linear unfolding of the plot
than to suggest any cyclical quality that might
be implied by the designated seasons, which,
with the year, serve to label the individual
chapters.

The novel itself opens with the beginning of
a break from the cycles of the past. Melech
Adler, the family patriarch and Noah's grandfather, calls a meeting to insist that the old
religious rules of the Adler family continue in
force. His sons have been frequenting a local
hangout even on Saturday. Relying on credit,
they have paid for their entertainment after the
holy day has passed and so have not technically
violated the proscription against doing any kind
of business on *shabus*—but only technically.
Melech maintains that "buying on credit was
only one step away from buying, and if a Jew
bought things on the sabbath he might as well go
without a hat, and if a Jew went without a hat he
might as well miss the evening prayer, and if a
Jew missed the evening prayer . . ." (ellipsis in the
original). It all hangs together in a way. But the
family does not. The sons hypocritically accept
the dicta of the father even though they no
longer believe them. The youngest son, to whom

the meeting was especially addressed, is already irretrievably embarking on a course of delinquency—delinquencies rather more serious than not keeping *shabus*. The grandchildren find Melech increasingly irrelevant to their lives, and Noah, the oldest of the them, the oldest son of Melech's oldest son and formerly the old man's favorite, is conspicuously absent from the family assembly. That absence signals Noah's revolt. He has left the Montreal ghetto, left his family, taken a room of his own. *Son of a Smaller Hero* is the story of Noah's flight from an order of life, that of the Orthodox Jew, that was itself fast disappearing.

Noah flees from the conventional restraint of narrowly defined religious and social strictures. What he flees to is conventional also. His first fumblings toward independence are a low-level job and the beginning of a middle-level education. At Wellington College (based on Montreal's Sir George Williams College), Noah encounters Theo Hall, a consciously and conscientiously good man who works hard to upgrade the small college at which he teaches. Hall, however, despite his concern for education and good literature, is a desperately empty man. The first sign of that emptiness is an inordinate desire for disciples. Noah, of course, is soon cast in the role of prospective protégé. He is to be the recipient—and the proof—of Hall's goodness. Theo even insists that Noah come and live with him and Mrs. Hall. Since Miriam Hall is a woman who possesses a repressed "Desire for Life" that renders her not-so-secretly dissatisfied with her not-so-satisfactory husband, since Theo Hall is little more than a stereotypical specimen of the sterile academic (and there are numerous hints in the novel as to his sexual shortcomings), it is a foregone conclusion that Noah and Miriam will soon share more than living quarters. Written determinedly from the point of view of the young rebel who takes the dissatisfied woman to his bed, the novel soon takes on the quality of a fairy tale, and the husband's poor apprentice casts himself, not incongruously, as the wife's rescuing prince.

Of course this fairy tale cannot end happily for Miriam. But it will be an important step in grooming the prince to be a king of another sort—that is, the modern, iconoclastic artist. Against her better judgment Miriam leaves the security provided by her husband and the status of being Mrs. Professor Hall for the more passionate love of the younger man. Almost immediately she begins to diminish in his eyes. When he first came to live with the Halls, Noah could think of nothing but Mrs. Hall. Whenever possible he would steal a glance at Miriam passing through the living room, then return to his own room, "his longing briefly nourished," and "lie down with a fresh and tender image of her all his own to manipulate in his mind." When the image is succeeded by the real thing, the vision dims. Images do not make demands. They do not worry that they are older than, and unmarried to, the man whose dream they are. Soon Miriam is, for Noah, merely a despondent woman approaching middle age, another dependent burden, and very like his mother. The young man who left his family for love must abandon love for freedom. An affair, Richler suggests, can be a ghetto too.

One of the smaller ironies of the novel is that Noah leaves his family and comes to live with Miriam and then leaves Miriam to return to his family. He returns to his family, of course, only to leave once more. Noah's second decision to embark for freedom is even more difficult than the first one, since it is made soon after his father's death and in the face of his mother's prospective death (she has already suffered one heart attack and is sure that her son's impending second departure will cause another and fatal attack). Since Noah must twice make the painful choice of self over family, we should forgive his choice of self over Miriam. For surely she, too, seeing the difficult decisions that he makes, must understand how important it is for the young man to leave them all, herself included.

Miriam should understand Noah for still another reason. His story, and his abandonment of her, partly recapitulates her story, and her abandonment of Theo. She too sought to escape the limitations of her past, her poverty as a child. When the first escape, her marriage to Theo, proves to be mostly another trap, she must flee it too. But when the second escape does not prove final, does not fulfill all the promises anticipated, Miriam returns, completely defeated, to the marriage that had already been found wanting. Her state then is worse than it was before Noah arrived on the scene, as shown by the compulsive affairs she conducts at the end of the novel. These infidelities, enacted almost in the presence of both her husband and his dominating mother, make a mockery of any pretense to marriage. We see, in short, a graphic illustration of the high cost of a faked commitment to family, which is to say that Miriam, as one principal actor in Noah's story, provides a partial parallel by which Noah can be judged. Had he permanently returned to St. Lawrence Street, to be taken in by the Adlers, to live in reluctant half-compliance with his mother's plans for her *boyele*, he would have been as much a failure as Miriam.

Other characters in the novel also partly parallel Noah and at the same time provide the image of what he should not become. Shloime, Melech's youngest son, is particularly pertinent in this respect. Uncle and nephew are approximately the same age. Both think of themselves as the young in opposition to the old. Both translate their opposition into action. Shloime at one point even insists to Noah that, considering their fondness for married non-Jewish women and nonkosher food, they have "got a lot in common." But Shloime's revolt against Orthodoxy descends to a direct attack on the family when he sets fire to Melech's coal yard. Gauged against the measure of the dishonest and destructive Shloime, Noah's rebellion is necessary and good. Noah's search for values—"he was hungering for an anger or a community or a traditon to which he could relate his experience"—also obviously contrasts to Shloime's. Noah is impelled toward art, philosophy, a hard-won personal morality, freedom. Shloime finally finds all of his answers to any "Problems of Life" in the army. There he is treated well and trained to kill the "Commies," who are, he is told, threatening his country.

Noah's father dies in the fire Shloime sets. That death marks a crucial point in the life of Noah. First, the tragedy conveniently provides a dramatic occasion whereby Noah can break away from the woman he did not know how to leave. But the death of Wolf Adler also raises crucial psychological and moral questions for the son. He is brought back into the family and into contact with the various possibilities of life that his various uncles represent. We have already noted Shloime and the criminal rebellion that he embodies. At the other end of the spectrum is Itzik, the most Orthodox of Melech's sons, who also represents a nonviable option for Noah. It is this uncle who is especially critical of Noah, almost pugnaciously so. Even while Wolf's body is being dug out from the rubble after the coal yard fire, Itzik vociferously condemns Noah for drinking too much, for not wearing the yarmulka, for the *goyishe* girlfriend. Realizing that Itzik desperately defends a way of life that is on the verge of extinction, Noah avoids a fight and allows the insults and innuendos to wash over him, a definite sign that he has passed from late adolescent vociferous rebellion to a more fundamental, philosophical rebellion that has, at its base, a deeply humanistic spirit.

Noah, however, cannot be urbanely magnanimous when another uncle, Max, who is running for alderman, wants to exploit the bogus beatification of Wolf Adler for his own political purposes. Noah discovered his father's body, beneath the rubble of the yard office shack and in front of many witnesses. When the charred remains were found, Wolf's hand was still in a box belonging to Melech Adler, a box that usually remained under lock and key in the office safe. Wolf, we know, thought that the box contained cash. Noah finds, however, only laboriously copied religious scrolls and a bundle of old yellowed letters along with a few faded photographs of a plump, blond young woman and some ancient receipts. Realizing that those latter papers are his "inheritance," he pockets them to examine them later. Then, when the box still containing the scrolls is handed over to Melech—who had insisted that if the box were found it was not to be touched—a bystander grabs it to see for himself what the fuss was all about. Immediately the cry goes up, "Wolf Adler died for the Torah." Sainthood is assured. Wolf's funeral is attended by thousands that never knew the pathetic man who really died from greed. Ironically, the pointless death makes him a hero, if only a "smaller" one.

Max, the shrewdest of the brothers, soon realizes that Wolf was no Jewish hero. Max also faces a hard election. The coffin of a man "who died for the Torah" makes a great campaign platform. Noah, who also knows that Wolf's new status is undeserved, demurs, and dignifies his father's death by insisting on at least a measure of the truth. Unless Max drops Wolf's name from his ad campaign, Noah will reveal to the press and the public that the youngest brother set the fire. "My brother Wolf, defender of the faith," will win votes; "my brother Shloime, arsonist and fratricide," will not. Max drops the issue, and so does Noah. The point here is that Noah counters and forestalls another version of himself, the calculating operator. He also shows that he can strike a balance even as the proponent of the truth. He does not, for example, insist to his mother—who finally has become a respected "lady" in the Jewish community—that Wolf Adler was a would-be thief, and neither does he point out to Melech, the stern proponent of harsh truth and unforgiving justice, that it was really the youngest son and not the hated *goyim* who set the fire in which the oldest son perished.

Wolf's dubious death allows for one of the most effective scenes in the novel, the account of his grand funeral. Since that funeral is a kind of party in celebration of Wolf Adler's ersatz heroism, Richler appropriately bases his description on the description of the one large party that paid tribute to Gatsby's pseudo-greatness in Fitzgerald's classic novel. The rhythms and the details are interchangeable, once we remove the markings of class and occasion. Names like Yosel Wiserman, Simcha Rabinovitch, Estelle Geiger, Art Gold, Benjy Tulch, Moishe the Idiot—each attached to an appropriate aphorism or anecdote—are all blended together in a colorful portrait of the protagonist's milieu, a milieu in which he now stands apart as the alien and the observer. It is also at the funeral that eight of the

central characters give, in turn, their silent musings on the meaning of Wolf's death. In each
case what is presented is really an apology for
the life of the mourner. Max begins, "Me, I put
my trust in Dow Jones." Itzik brags that "I know
more about the laws than any of the boys. Ask
Paw." The assimilationist Harry Goldenberg
proclaims, "We go forward two steps, then along
come . . . Thank God, Alger Hiss was a Gentile."
Leah still clings to the dream that her father was
a Zaddick and begins to proclaim that her long-
lamented match to Wolf was really "made in
heaven." Her father was apparently "a prophet
after all." Even Noah joins the chorus with a
simple epiphany: "I am thankful, Daddy, that if
you were here you would have had the good
sense to have turned your back on it." Praise,
however, soon gives way to paradox, as the son
muses on how little his father had ever been
praised: "Ironic that you who suffered all your
life for what people said should not be capable of
hearing them when they, the people, are at last
saying fine things about you."

   With Wolf's death Noah comes, symbolically if not literally, into his own inheritance.
That inheritance is, first, the record of his
grandfather's secret life. But one uncovered
record is soon followed by a second. Beneath the
false bottom of the bottom drawer of his desk,
Wolf Adler also concealed secret papers, his
"Strictly Private" diary, in which he set forth his
"Memories—Prospects—Inventions and Thoughts."
The diary is also in code, code that is pathetically
transparent. Deciphering this document does

not give Noah any new perspective on his father.
But it does bring some old truths home to him in
palpable form: his father's foolish dreams
("There was a project to build a bridge across the
Atlantic"); the tedium of his life as proved by
what he chose to record ("Another page listed
Wolf's weight before and after eating, before and
after defecation"). Most depressing of all, every
quarrel with Leah has been entered. And ave-
raged: "Average over a twenty-year period—2.2
quarrels per day"—the sad history of a marriage.

In the case of both hidden accounts, the
meaning is the same. Neither Melech nor Wolf
was fully his own man. In each case the secret
record attests to limitations not acknowledged
by the public face. In each case the message to
Noah is also the same. To what degree will he be
the continuation of his grandfather's and his
father's lives. Will he too follow a course that he
can justify in his own eyes only by postulating a
hidden, other, might-have-been existence? Or
will he avoid that questionable division and
avoid it partly because he can see how it was for
them, because he can embrace, in both father
and grandfather, the public and the private
man? It is at this point that we can see how much
Noah must accept *and* deny his forebears, in
contrast to his earlier, simpler, less convincing,
and less conclusive denial when he simply left
home and moved in with Miriam.

It is also at this point that we can see how
much Noah stands in obvious contrast to another main character in the novel, his mother.
Leah Goldenberg Adler could neither accept nor

reject the men in her life. And, instead of hiding away the divisions on which her existence turns, she loudly proclaims them to all who will listen. So she praises her father as the saintly Zaddik and laments the marriage that he arranged for her. She tells Noah of his grandfather's wise words to all who would listen and also tells the grandson of the pathetic falsehood with which the old man died. He vainly hoped that there would be some sign of his sainthood, a light, as he expired. She told him that there was and then tried to live the lie of his death by affirming the sainthood that rested mostly on her compassionate lie. The daughter of this other smaller hero thereby endures a bitterly unhappy marriage to a man who is, she believes, her social and intellectual inferior, and her solace in that marriage is to try to align the son with her against his father. This process does not require the cooperation of the son. So Noah left them, she insists to Wolf early in the novel, "because *you're* common" whereas she is "a lady" (emphasis in the original). Yet, when Wolf dies supposedly a hero, Leah embraces in death the man and the marriage that she could not endure in life, and also sets out to cast Noah in a new unlikely role. He will be an ideal son-cum-husband/husband-cum-son. He will fulfill her dreams by acting, she insists, to fulfill dreams that are also, she insists, his own. How much better he will do at McGill than his cousin Harvey, her brother's son. The hypocrisy of this whole venture is perfectly summed up in Leah's reaction to Noah's final refusal to have any part in it as positively demonstrated by his impending departure for Europe:

> "I'll write you every week, Maw."
> "Write, don't write. To put a knife into my back would have been kinder. Now go. Go. Be happy."

As that quote indicates, Leah is, in some respects, the standard caricature of the Jewish mother and a master at manipulating through applied guilt. Noah, moreover, is especially susceptible to manipulation immediately after his father's demise because of his own sense of double guilt. He partly blames himself—"a blindly selfish bastard" of a son—for his father's death. Furthermore, the cause and expression of his selfishness, the affair with Miriam, has gone badly. Indeed, he comes close to falling into a trap that would be the reverse of his grandfather's mistake. Melech would not marry the "wrong girl," but he continued to love her. Noah was willing to marry the wrong girl, even though he had ceased to love her. To validate his past affair, to prove it was not just the young man's fling that it so clearly was, Noah proposes. Only Miriam's pride—she recognizes the grounds for the proposal and how she would be used, even in his attempt to satisfy himself that he was not using her—forestalls another disastrous mistake. But that forestalling again emphasizes Noah's guilt: " 'I'll be able to forgive you everything in time,' she said. 'Except your having to get drunk. Except your having asked me to marry you.' "

It would be tempting to retreat, at this point, to the safety of a life managed by mother, and

Noah does briefly try to show that in at least one role, that of *boyele*, he can measure up. But to his credit—and this is largely what he gains from the legacy of his father's and grandfather's contrary example—Noah cannot long hide from himself the duplicity of his return to faith and family. Being a good son, befriending his cousins, courting a nice Jewish girl, he is only playing at assimilation. He also sees that the play, as obvious play, defeats its immediate ostensible objective: "Noah was so intent on conforming that he conformed too much, and was suspected as an eccentric, a non-believer, by all." He sees too that all those around him play a similar game that is simply less obvious:

He finally realized that the secret of their humanity was that each one had a tiny deviation all his and/or her own. None conformed completely. Marsha [his recent "steady"], the little bitch, had love being made to her by a McGill quarterback whilst she was trying to hook Noah. (That finally endeared her to him.) His Aunt Rachel obeyed in all things except that she secretly read the most blatantly pornographic literature, and Mrs. Feldman beat her French poodle with a whip.

And because these others play more successfully (i.e., less self-consciously) than Noah, they also remain much more the prisoners of their games. The previously quoted passage continues: "Terror lurked behind their happiness. In fact, they weren't happy at all: they were composed. Truth was adroitly side-stepped, like a dog's excrement on the footpath." Only Noah

sees that such play should end. Noah also begins
to see the larger implications of such private
play. In each case the covert rebellion against a
self-imposed or self-confirmed definition effectively precludes any real questioning of the definition itself. In much that same vein, we also
see various Jewish characters kicking at the
walls of the ghetto and thereby confirming the
existence of the ghetto. Noah, with his first
departure, kicked at the walls. With his second,
he jumps over them.

   He cannot depart, however, until the final
confrontation with Melech, which is psycholo-
gically and narratively the real climax of the
novel. Indeed, much of the novel is structured
around the relationship between grandfather
and grandson. The first main episode in the plot,
it will be remembered, was the family counsel
called by Melech, which Noah had refused to
attend. Into the description of that meeting
Richler interjects a flashback that tells of the
first and crucial break between Noah and
Melech. From an early age, Noah was the ador-
ing grandson. As we learn later, Melech refuses
to make his first son, Noah's father, a partner in
his business or even an heir to his fortune—distinctions that he apparently wished to bestow,
instead, on the grandson. But one day, when
Noah accompanies his idolized grandfather to
the coal yard he witnesses what, to his eleven-
year-old mind, is a shocking case of dishonesty—dishonesty, finally, on the part of his
grandfather. While Melech entertains in his
office a man selling scrap metal, Noah observes

that the workers have failed to weigh all of the metal being sold. The boy then persists in his attempts to tell his grandfather of the "mistake" until Melech slaps him. The child runs away; the grandfather runs after, trying to explain that "the goy" had stolen the scrap himself, some of it from Melech, and had tried to cheat Melech in other ways too.[2] Noah refuses to listen or to understand. From then on there is a gulf between them.

The two are only driven further apart when Noah finds the packet of letters. Earlier it was the young boy who could not resolve the difference between the two views of what his grandfather seemed to be. In the second crisis, however, it is Melech who cannot bridge the difference between what he wants to seem—the stern, righteous patriarch—and what he is afraid he will seem to be after Noah reads the letters. That latter fear represents his own judgment of himself. He had left Miss Helga Kubalski, but he could never fully believe that he had rightly done so, as shown by the money he sent up to the outbreak of World War II, as shown by the letters he goes on writing but does not post up to just a few days before the fire. Unable to accept, or reject, his judgment on himself, he turns his anger on Noah, whom he condemns as a thief and whom he charges not to see him again, not even at his funeral.

The final meeting of Noah and Melech occurs at a crucial point for both of them. Noah has broken off the relationship with Miriam and he has just told his mother goodbye. He has tried to be kind in both cases, and the kindness has failed miserably. Furthermore, Noah is already being charged with his mother's impending death from her weak heart.[3] Still he leaves, not knowing if the heart condition is real—in which case his leaving might kill her—or a sign of her own neurosis and her ruse to trap him forever in a deadly life. Melech, on the other hand, has felt a momentary desire to be comforted by his daughter. He goes to look into her room and sees that she is dancing naked with an invisible partner. "His eyes blurred. *Helga, Helga, forgive me.*" His daughter turns to see her father staring at her, and he sees himself seen as a voyeur. "His shoulders slumped. He was surprised and ashamed that his daughter could think of him in such a foul way." He tries to turn silently away, but she rails at him of his unkindness, of how happy she will be when she leaves him. He is an old man, crushed, when Noah comes to return the purloined letters.

Noah, coming to say goodbye, also wants to apologize for having taken the letters. Melech counters with condemnation—"You are by me de greatest shame I had. Go"—even though he desperately wants to confide in the boy, to make the boy respect him. A family patriarch but a petty man, he is afraid that Noah might admire the father more than the grandfather. Yet he overcomes his jealousy and his dedication to harsh truth enough to provide Noah with a compassionate falsehood: "Your Paw knew that I had in the box scrolls. About the other stuff he didn't know. Nobody knew." Noah understands the truth of the lie and returns the favor by not telling the grandfather who really started the fire. Both gifts, however, are covert, and Melech still cannot face the fact of Helga:

"Go, become a *Goy*. But have one look first at what the *Goyim* did to your *Zeyda*. That girl in the picture had she been willing to become a Jewess, to . . . Stones they threw at me, Noah. My heart they made hard against my children. Who burned me down my office? Who murdered my first-born? *Goyim*. *Goyim*. Now go. Go. Go join, become my enemy."

Melech has to have the *goyim* and the ghetto as his excuse for being Melech. Yet the letters and the scrolls, both written when there was no one but Melech to read them, testify to another side, a deeper pain. Noah asks for one of the scrolls his grandfather had copied. Wolf Adler died for the Torah. No. But Noah Adler leaves the ghetto armed with the Torah, with a blessing that his grandfather covertly gives even as he overtly denies doing so. The winter ending, Melech certain that *his* God (created "in his own image"), "stern, sometimes just, and always without mercy, would . . . punish the boy," does not cancel out the promise of hope also set forth at the conclusion of the novel. Noah does depart for his new life with his grandfather's grudging approval.

The book reverberates with surprising depths, and the characters have a complexity that was nowhere evident in *The Acrobats*. Noah, Melech, and Wolf are complex individuals effectively portrayed and effectively deployed.

Their strained familial relationships are believable, as the differently strained relationships in *The Acrobats* are not. I earlier noted that *Son of a Smaller Hero* has been viewed as Richler's second *first* novel. But I would here maintain that, even as a *second* first novel, the work still shows how far the young author had come from his *first* first one. Most obviously, in the second novel, the balances work. We see the various ways in which Noah is pulled, the conflicting claims that are put on him, and the impossibility of fairly and finely resolving them all. Because the characters and their actions are well realized, there is no need for a literary striving for effect. The book is not overwritten. As the last quotations, Melech's words to his grandson and his musings to himself, should indicate, Richler perfectly captures the tone and nuances of his characters.

Which is not to say that the novel is without faults. Some clichés do persist. Leah is too much the standard domineering Jewish mother. Her heart attack the moment her *boychuk* leaves is perhaps too contrived. Miriam, after Noah has left her, predictably stumbles from meaningless affair to meaningless affair, unable to find satisfaction in substitutes now that she has experienced the Real Thing. And, also true to standard form, the weak academic, Theo Hall, merely watches his wife destroy herself and their marriage, while his manipulating mother (a testimony to what Mrs. Adler might have become?) happily watches them both pay the price for Theo's involvement with a woman other than herself. Finally, Noah is an admittedly engaging protagonist, but he does not fully merit the sympathy with which he is portrayed.

Such faults, however, are easily outweighed by the book's numerous virtues—virtues that were not present in *The Acrobats*. So if the first novel gives us Richler's first handling of most of his characteristic themes, the second book gives us his first characteristic presentation of these same themes. In its probing of family relationships and the strained connections between individuals who come from different backgrounds, classes, and traditions, in its assessment of the duty of the individual to the individual, as opposed to other conflicting duties, and, finally, in its examination of the mechanics of exile, this work looks forward to subsequent novels like *A Choice of Enemies* and *The Apprenticeship of Duddy Kravitz*, but even more so to the still later works, *St. Urbain's Horseman* and *Joshua Then and Now*.

4

Politics, Love, and Loss:
A Choice of Enemies

Noah Adler, toward the end of *Son of a Smaller Hero*, "realized, at last, that . . . he had been defining himself Against." He had discovered what "he did Not Want," not what he did. The first discovery, of course, is a necessary prerequisite for the second and often leads to it. Noah, moreover, is only twenty-one—an appropriate age to be rebelling against the patterns into which others would fit him. The title of Richler's third novel, *A Choice of Enemies*, suggests that we will have again a similar plot and see once more a protagonist begin to find out what he is by choosing what he is against. But Norman Price, the main character in *A Choice of Enemies*, is no Noah Adler. To begin with, Norman is thirty-eight and quite too old to play the ingénue, the young man first encountering life on his own. Norman, moreover, has already fulfilled several dreams common to his generation. He has been a war hero, a university teacher, a writer. So the problem is not to find a viable dream—or, harder, to realize it. Norman's problem is even more difficult; he must learn to live on the far side of the dream, to live with the realization that what he lived for in the past did not really amount to very much. In short, Richler may have stalled slightly at the beginning of his career and given us two novels that were too obviously works of the author as a young man, but with his third book he matured markedly.[1] Although *A Choice of Enemies* does have some weaknesses, Richler is still in control of his material and presents it with the rigorous yet generous objectivity that has continued to characterize his best work.

The delicate balance of the objectivity saves a novel that at several points could easily have gone astray. Essentially, *A Choice of Enemies* is the story of a man middle-aged in years and experience but still young in expectation. Norman Price is also very much a man of his time. In opposition to the prevailing McCarthyism in the United States, he leaves that country after losing his position as a university English teacher and comes to England where he pursues the profession of writing in a distinctly dilettantish fashion. But his first choice of postwar enemies (and, by extension, friends) soon requires realignment. Norman meets Sally MacPherson, a Canadian woman just entering her twenties, and falls in love with her. Sally, however, presently decides that she is in love with Ernst Haupt, an East German of her own age and also a recent immigrant to England. When Norman tries to play patron to the young lovers, he finds that the other members of the small community to which he belongs will not accept Ernst, whereupon he divorces himself from his former friends.

Norman's London associates are mostly Jewish, are almost all in England because of their communist sympathies; Ernst is German, has fled from the communist state of East Germany. As Sonny Winkleman, the main spokesman for the small expatriate circle and a man who was successful in Hollywood before he was blacklisted, puts it, "Look, Norm, in this world you've got to make a choice of enemies or you just can't live. The boy stands for everything you and I are against. Haven't we suffered enough for our beliefs without bending over ass-backwards to help the other side?" Norman sees that Winkleman's devotion to principle—"Freedom of speech. Freedom to believe in what you like"—really is "Freedom for Winkleman to speak. Freedom for Winkleman to believe what he likes." Norman chooses Ernst, chooses "Freedom." Or thinks he does. The issues, Richler shows, are all more complicated than his protagonist first imagines, and the book is rather more than a satire on the reactionary private values of professed public radicals.

To make the novel more than a timely political satire of the fifties, Richler gives the plot an unlikely twist. Early in Part One, Norman's younger brother, Nicky, is killed in Germany during a pointless and unnecessary fight with a young German refugee whom Nicky had earlier attempted to befriend. The killer, as we might expect, turns out to be Ernst Haupt. Norman discovers this fact soon after he makes his stand on behalf of Ernst. In short, his principles are tested more seriously than he intended. Nicky

was killed, for all practical purposes, in self-
defense. Yet it was Nicky who was killed. Furthermore, this especially beloved younger brother
lost his life at a party celebrating his twenty-first
birthday. It is a death, Norman decides, that
must be avenged. So the second choice of enemies is followed by a third. Norman, determined at first even to "kill" Ernst (who has now
become the "little Nazi"), turns away from his
previous principles in order to pursue his new
enemy, and that enemy will not abide Norman's
conception of justice anymore than Norman
would abide Winkleman's.

We must see in Norman both his strength
and weaknesses. He is a man of principle and
generous in his treatment of others, particularly
Sally and Ernst. That he can rise above his disappointment in love is to his credit. But that he
was unable to accept the circumstances of
Nicky's death should not be surprising. Nicky
was his brother, and Ernst has been his rival in
love. We should also view the other characters,
particularly Ernst, in the same broad, overall
fashion. None of them is a stock figure; all have
their own very human mixture of virtues and
defects. So just as the possible melodramatic
twisting of the plot precludes a simple political
satire, so too does the rounded portrayal of the
characters keep the novel from descending into
melodrama.

This briefly noted disjunction between plot
and character is, I would maintain, the most
problematic feature of the novel, and as such
should be considered more fully. It could even

be argued that the division is so deep that *A Choice of Enemies* almost necessarily sustains a choice of evaluations. The novel can be seen as primarily a subtle portrayal of symbolically suggestive characters, characters who—as both unique individuals and representative specimens—are deployed in a carefully controlled drama. How appropriate that the émigrés from the West, refugees from the American McCarthyism of the fifties, meet in London an émigré from the East, a young man who finds the new communism as distasteful as the old National Socialism. We hear frankly bourgeois North American writers and moviemakers in exile from Hollywood because of their communist proclivities, past or present, assert their dedication to freedom of thought and to the cause of the masses; we see them reject out of hand the "little bastard," the "little goon," the "little Nazi punk," who has definitely sprung from the masses but who refuses to be a communist. We also see among these exiles, most of whom are Canadian, one good man. But here Richler's ironic character portrayal becomes particularly pointed. Norman Price, the protagonist, is kind, considerate, decent in his dealings with almost everyone. The antagonist, Ernst Haupt, is crude and callow, is guilty of lying, stealing, killing. Yet Richler also shows that in the large questions they jointly confront, Norman fails as a human being and Ernst succeeds. In short, *A Choice of Enemies* gives us an ironically subtle vision of these men and their times:

It is a novel of the aftermath of conflict when blood has dried, bills must be footed, men measured; when the delayed shock of self discovery spreads havoc among the certainties of combat, for this is a novel of the end of ideologies.[2]

The complex vision of the novel is conveyed, unfortunately, through a dubious plot. We are asked to believe that Ernst, passing through West Germany, kills a young soldier in self-defense and then flees to England to encounter, as a friend, a patron, and a rival in a love triangle, the very brother of the man he killed. Indeed, the love triangle itself is a product of the killing. Norman, grieving over the death of his brother, temporarily abandons Sally, the new object of his affections, to seek solace in France and Spain. When he returns, he finds that the girl whom he had decided, while away, to marry has, while he was away, set up housekeeping with Ernst. Furthermore, during the course of the action Norman suffers a convenient bout of amnesia, and the novel itself is resolved by two unintended marriages, one unintended suicide, and a chance heroic rescue of an elderly Jewish man, actions that are all pulled out of the blue in the last few chapters. Such a resolution well might seem to creak with contrivance.

These two divergent assessments of the novel can be partly harmonized by arguing that the central "strained" coincidence simply demonstrates the existentialist's credo of absurdity. In an absurd world it is foolish to demand probability from either life or fiction. And just as Richler's two earlier novels have hints of

Hemingway and Fitzgerald, this one pays obvious tribute to Sartre and Camus. Set in post–World War II Europe, written by an author who had recently spent considerable time in both Paris and London, the book, as Pierre Cloutier observes, "brings the Canadian innocent abroad to share, reluctantly, in the destruction of a European illusion."[3] There are, of course, some North American illusions lost too. Ernst and Norman act out a drama illustrating "the moral bankruptcy" of the "European revolutionary tradition."[4] They also invalidate the essentially New World theme of new love, new life, a new start.

In the early part of the novel, Norman envisions a new life with Sally. But, ironically, he would both make his fresh start in the Old World and make it slowly. Ernst, it should be noted, enters the picture because Norman prefers a reserved and private commitment to the woman of his choice. Despite her obvious feelings for him, he is from the first concerned mostly with the appearance of propriety. Can a man old enough to know better look like he is trying to seduce the "sweetheart of Sigma something." The answer for Norman is "no," and so he holds Sally at arm's length, even though he dreams of love and marriage. In their one close encounter with sex, the young woman takes by far the more active role. Norman is saved by the bell; he is completely put off by a badly timed telephone call and then is retrospectively relieved that nothing happened. The telephone call was for him; it told him that a telegram had just arrived. The telegram tells him of his brother's death. When he leaves London the next morning for the solace of the Continent, he does not tell Sally that he is going; during the some four weeks that he is away, he sends her only one postcard. In short, he insists on stalling and indecision. Furthermore, he does not even have the courage of his own lack of convictions. The one friend in whom he has confided his feelings for Sally has to explain to him what he is doing: "So you're going to use your brother's death as an excuse for running away." Ernst, the cause of that running away, turns out to be the consequence too. Norman, by not clearly choosing Sally, in effect chooses Ernst for her.

After he has thrown Sally to whomever will catch her, Norman laments his loss. "Why had he fled Sally?" But then he perhaps has pretty much what he has wanted all along, as is suggested by the way he remains at hand to enjoy it. He tells himself that henceforward he "must keep [his] life free of disturbances." Nevertheless, and despite his determination to return to the Continent, he remains in London, living next door to the lovers and serving as their protector and patron. Richler manages to set up this situation without casting Norman as a sexually neurotic secret voyeur (that role is played by another character in the novel, Karp) or as a man enamoured of his own magnanimity. The inauthentic choices that Norman makes toward the end of the novel are much simpler. But they are deployed in such a fashion that they magnify their own inauthenticity and finally add up to a self-created *enfers* from which, for Norman, all ways are closed.

One should not overemphasize, however, the existential element in the novel. Again there are countering balances, for Richler retreats from the conventions—already, in the fifties, becoming clichés—of the novel of absurdity even as he employs them. We can note, for example, how he gives a psychological motivation to his existentialist "anti-hero." Norman has a case history, something that Mersault, in *L'Etranger*, has not, for the prosecuting attorney's attempts to explain Mersault are totally specious. Not so in Norman's case. He is a contemporary dangling man who would avoid emotional disturbances, not because he embodies the human condition, but because he has not sufficiently recovered from an accident of war—the shelling of his RCA fighter plane, his subsequent crash, and the consequent occasional amnesia. Emotional stress brings on new attacks; that recurring problem both symbolizes his isolation and partly explains it. He is reluctant to inflict himself on others or others on himself.[5] This case history particularizes Norman, makes the reader sympathize with him, but also differentiates *A Choice of Enemies* from other existential fictions of the fifties.

The book seems to be, in part, an existentialist fable and, in part, a realistic novel that verges on social satire. Again the novel seems in conflict with itself. The two forms do not normally go together. Existentialist fable emphasizes the fundamental absurdity of life. Satire, however, and particularly realistic satire, is posited on the assumption that the absurd is not fundamental but is amenable to rational control. Thus the London émigrés all come to a dawning awareness that, as fellow travelers, they had been considerably misled by Stalin. Clearly, there were lessons to be learned. The others could well follow Norman and achieve some larger perspective on their complacent state of exile too. Yet Ernst poses essentially the same social and moral questions in a much broader perspective but to a different point:

"A brother and sister in Munich distributed pamphlets against Hitler during the war. They were shot as traitors. After the war they were resurrected as heroes. Today they are traitors again."

"I'm not listening."

"When your Ike came into Germany and saw the camps he said we shall never forget this. Ten years later the same Ike said—"

"I don't care," she said. "I don't hear a word."

"There is no right or wrong. There are conditions, rewards, punishments, and sides, but that's all."

And what is the clear moral lesson here? Norman too has occasional glimmerings of this larger perspective that calls all private principles and political platforms into question:

Around him the real £ s.d. world existed. The only sons of white fathers went out to Malaya to murder the only sons of yellow fathers in the interests of national prestige. . . . Around him moved a real city where Sally's choice of a lover, Charlie's script, Winkleman's chance of a production, and his own loneliness were of no bloody account.

In the passages just quoted both Ernst and Norman are, on one level, right. On another, they are not. Richler's growing maturity as a novelist is especially indicated by the effective way in which he juxtaposes and even juggles levels. The novel is made up of countering perspectives, of seemingly disparate elements. On the lowest level, the book is about the self-aggrandizing close-mindedness of the leftist expatriates in London. Nevertheless, Sally, when she first encounters them, can rightly praise the "instinctive generosity" of these same individuals: "There was plenty to be said for a group of men who, though they were naturally competitors and professionally jealous of each other's success, still did their utmost to share out the available work." Yet the quote continues: "But what astonished her was the ways in which the 'enlightened' left was similar to the less intelligent groups it despised. The loyalties, the generosity, like those of the Rotary, lost in purity by being confined to the group strictly." She is quite right here too and also when she concludes "that Norman and his friends were not, as they supposed, non-conformists, but conformists to another rule." The oxymorons—selfish generosity, Rotarian revolutionaries, and conforming nonconformity—all apply. Norman is both the good man he tries to be and the bungler who brings unhappiness to those he attempts to help and who finally destroys, figuratively and literally, the woman he loves. Ernst is both the victim of circumstance and the active agent of his own disasters. He can at times hate himself for killing

Nick; at other times he pleads extenuating circumstances and insists he acted only in self-defense; once he even proudly points out that Sally is much more immorally prone to moral casuistry than he is: " 'To you the fact that I killed Nicky ... has become an inconvenience, no more. But me,' he shouted, 'I'm the Hitler youth scum. Oh, you big, wonderful moral people. Is this what I've been missing?' " Each reaction is understandable; each, within its context, rings true. It is that ring of truth that gives us, in this early novel, some of Richler's most fully realized characters.

Depth of character and complexity of moral vision go together throughout the novel. It is hard to judge even the most minor of characters, such as Ernst's father, who is only mentioned in passing as "wandering from zone to zone ... seeking something lost—his family and his self-respect." Karl Haupt's "legacy" that sent him wandering "was compounded of weakness and a dubious pride in the fact that he had objected to Hitler slightly, but not enough." He had resisted; but not much; but not much is still resisting. Or we can note how Bob Landis is portrayed early in the novel as the most shallow and insignificant of the expatriates. He is perpetually in pursuit of seductions and, as soon as the opportunity arises, makes an obligatory pass at Sally, even though she is supposedly Norman's girlfriend at the time. Yet he readily lends Norman his car, so that Norman can better conduct his own affair with Sally. Also, late in the novel, when Norman, who now "exuded [a] distinct ... odour of failure" just happens to drop by at the Landises on a night when they are having a party, Bob treats him with great consideration. He insists that they all go out for supper. Then, when Norman won't return to the house, Bob sends his wife back to greet the guests and stays with Norman drinking and talking. And in the course of that conversation he can also assert that he is "a humanist" and "believe[s] that human life is sacred," even as he wonders if Norman "might know of a safe abortionist." Present kindness has not superseded previous philandering. Sally, with Ernst fled, has now been left to Bob. She has become pregnant and wants to bear the baby. He insists on an abortion. To win her way, she decides on a faked attempted suicide. "Melodramatic deceit . . . was in his idiom." He will rightly misunderstand, she calculates, the gesture that she does not at all mean. But that is the evening when Norman visits Bob; Bob, normally most punctual, arrives at Sally's apartment much later than expected; the pretend suicide turns real.

A Choice of Enemies, as "a novel at the end of ideologies," shows political programs to be even more pointless and self-defeating than personal ones. Ernst remembers that when his father "had at last been picked up for questioning in Saxony the communist police official turned out to be the same one who had used to question him for the Nazis." The liberation of postwar Europe in a nutshell. Or, as Ernst puts essentially the same proposition to Norman when "on principle" Norman insists that he

cannot accept the other's explanation of the
killing of Nicky and must turn him over to the
police: " 'Your kind, your generation, you killed
for ideals, principles, and a better world. . . . Hitler burned the Jews,' Ernst shouted, 'and Stalin
murdered the kulaks, all so that there should be
a better world for me.' " Deceit, self-deception,
the novel suggests, are the human condition. The
émigrés who during the course of the novel hold
a committee-on-unexpatriate-activities hearing
regarding Norman's loyalty to their cause and,
with dubious evidence, find him guilty are not
much better than the communist hunters who
hounded them from America.

They are not much better and certainly they
are no worse. The friends who condemn Norman
were themselves formerly in much higher places.
Betraying their friendship with Norman even as
they investigate him as a betrayer of friends,
they play at having an importance they no longer
possess. Who can be surprised if that play is
closely modeled on the play that undid them.
Furthermore, it was all an exercise in "illusion,"
and afterwards they are mostly all "ashamed" of
the way they have treated Norman, who, incidentally, suffers no real loss at their hands. Not
even Charlie Lawson, the friend who manufac-
tures the case against Norman, can be convincingly condemned. He informs on a man to whom
he should be especially grateful. But that is
precisely the problem. Norman has been too ac-
commodating to this friend, giving up his own
living quarters for Charlie and his wife, arranging writing jobs for Charlie, allowing Charlie to

believe that Norman had once tried to seduce Charlie's wife, Joey, instead of the other way around. When that deception finally ends, Charlie admits to his wife what he has been feeling all along: " 'Big, honest, principled Norman. If he had made love to you—Oh, if you only knew how much I wanted to have something on him . . .' " Gratitude galls.

Charlie, Joey, and Norman comprise one triangle in the novel. Sally, Ernst, and Norman make up another. The subsidiary triangle balances the major one, a balance that helps to give structure to the book. In each triangle Norman fulfills the role of patron, protector, the good man, and in each he is finally the odd man out. The two triangles also have their differences. With Charlie and Joey, Norman plays his self-defined role comfortably, at no cost to himself. So he plays it comparatively honestly. Joey and Charlie are the characters who slip into occasional "bad faith." With Sally and Ernst, just the opposite situation obtains. Norman befriends the two because that friendship allows him to remain close to Sally, whom he more and more (but characteristically too late) decides he loves. In this threesome, it is Norman's role that is difficult and that encourages various deceptions. When he goes to considerable trouble to help the two of them, arranging, for example, for Ernst's immigration to Canada, this is not the same generous kindness that he showered on the Lawsons. His one solace in disappointment is his persistent underhanded attempt to demonstrate to Sally that he really is the better man. And with

Ernst his friendship is even more obviously
two-faced. Thus he can invite Ernst to the party
given by his writer and movie-producer friends,
knowing full well, but not consciously admitting
it to himself, that Ernst, quite out of his depth,
will undoubtedly make a fool of himself, which
Ernst does.

Sally and Ernst both act in better faith. They
each seek Norman's good opinion before the
dark truth of Nicky's death comes out. Afterwards, they both want his forgiveness. And here
the two triangles especially contrast. Charlie and
Joey, both losers in the first triangle, learn compassion. When their various self-deceptions come
to light, they find comfort in each other and thereby undo what would otherwise be two total
defeats. Norman, the loser in the second triangle,
cannot transcend his loss. When the way in
which he has been deceived (or more accurately,
what he sees as deception) comes to light, he
falls back on principle and insists he will turn
Ernst over to the police. Ernst suggests that the
principle is really love of Sally, and, moreover,
"if it had been the other way around," Norman
would have protected his brother and called that
"loyalty." Norman acknowledges both charges
but will not alter his intentions:

> "If I get twenty years you would have murdered
> me, just like I killed your brother. But at least I was
> being attacked. I had no choice, but you—"
> "I have no choice, either."

Both reverse the title of the book. A choice of
enemies becomes "no choice." Ernst, of course,

while "being attacked," had no real choice. But Norman is under no such compulsion when he falsely proclaims that he has no choice; his choice is Ernst as enemy. That choice shows how his principles can be as self-serving as anyone else's. He reacts contemptuously to his former friends when, for reasons that will not bear scrutiny, they merely lower their opinion of him. For reasons that will not bear scrutiny, he is ready to destroy Ernst's life.

Norman is not the only one to have problems defining Ernst. Indeed, the older brother recapitulates in more extended form basically the same process that the younger brother followed. Nicky, as an American soldier stationed in postwar Germany, "yearned to be recognized as something more personal than just another occupation soldier" (i.e., to be chosen as a friend and not an enemy). To achieve, at least on a low level, that worthy objective, he took up with Ernst. So there is a substantial element of role-playing on his part, just as there later is with Norman. Nicky, for example, proves his goodness by the large and unsolicited gift that he immediately gives Ernst, sixty of the hundred dollars that Norman has sent as a birthday present. In each case the relationship is also complicated by the fact that Ernst proceeds with less than total candor. Of course, we can hardly expect him to confess to Norman who he is, and the fashion in which he first wishes to mislead Nicky is really not that serious either. Ernst lifts the wallet of one of Nicky's American friends to return it later. He will pretend he rescued it from a

thieving prostitute—all as a favor to Nicky in
return for the money Nicky gave him. But he is
seen by another of Nicky's friends, a Jewish soldier who is more than ready to dislike the German and who reports the theft to Nicky. When
Ernst now produces the wallet he is not believed,
but neither will Nicky publicly repudiate his new
friend. So, like Norman later, the younger
brother professes a friendship in which he does
not fully believe. He also begins to see that the
price of his new friendship is the loss of old
friends. And then the sudden switch: when it is
reported, falsely, that Ernst, at Nicky's birthday
party, is upstairs rifling through the coats, Nicky
succumbs to "a sudden and uncontrollable
anger ... against Ernst's betrayal" and everything else ugly and imperfect in his life. Ernst,
suddenly embodying all evil, is truly the chosen
enemy. Armed with a broken beer bottle, Nicky
goes to confront him. The other shall be brought
to justice, Nicky has decided, with even less
capability for weighing what justice should en-
tail than Norman will later have when he
similarly bungles the same matter.

Nicky's choice of Ernst as enemy brings on
his tragic death, which, it should be noted, is a
tragedy for Ernst too. It is not so clear, however,
just what Norman's choice of Ernst as enemy
brings him, even though some consequences
such as the total and irrevocable loss of Sally are
obvious. Perhaps Norman does gain some perspective on himself and his situation when, immediately after the crucial discovery, he briefly

succumbs to amnesia and wanders the London streets. That nighttown journey shows him the same dark underside of the city that Charles Dickens portrayed in *Bleak House* or Joseph Conrad in *The Secret Agent*. Yet this tour strikes no political chords, which is perhaps another tribute to the ultimate limitations of the ostensibly good man. Near the end of the novel Norman at last sums up the, for him, meaning of it all:

If there was a time to man the barricades, Norman thought, then there is also a time to weed one's private garden.... I the enemy was no longer the boor in power on the right or the boor out of power on the left. All alliances had been discredited. ... So in this time of wrecks, Norman, at the age of thirty-nine, chose at last to lead a private life.

The Candide reference to cultivating one's private garden does not encourage confidence in the quality of Noman's epiphany. The novel has shown few gardens worthy of cultivation. Yet this prospectus for the future does contain one positive note. Norman, in the final sentences, renounces his pursuit of Ernst: "So wherever he is let him go in peace. Let him be."

Ernst is no longer the chosen enemy. Indeed, the whole passage, as a kind of manifesto in reverse, advocates the merits of not choosing. "All alliances [choice of friends or enemies] had been discredited." That realization, however, follows hard on the heels of the formation of a new alliance. The musings just quoted come during the course of a wedding reception. Norman has married Vivian. That London woman, in her late twenties and desperate for a husband, took him in while he was suffering from amnesia. After the amnesia passes, Norman allows Vivian to fill the void left by Ernst's flight and the loss of Sally, but then, after the need for such diversion passes, his decision to call off their relationship meekly turns into a proposal. By the simple matter of beating Norman to the truth—" 'I think we'd better stop seeing each other,' Vivian said suddenly. . . . 'You feel obligated to me because I took care of you while you were ill'"—she contrives to have him maintain that is not how he feels at all: "Norman fiddled anxiously with his glasses. 'Would you like to marry me?' he asked." She would, she does. So the marriage with which the novel concludes is not inconsistent with Norman's final philosophy. He would have decided—had he decided to decide—differently.

That nondecision does not bode well for the future, even though one critic has seen the last episode as Norman heeding "the simple call of a wife, a child, and work."[6] His new wife, Norman realizes, "dismayed" during the reception, is a small-minded person who puffs him up to put down, with "malice" and "cruel intent," her old associates who did not properly appreciate her. She also immediately informs him that she is not at all ready to bear the child he wants to father at once. She lets him know, too, what his subsequent work should be. He has been taken in hand. Norman, indeed, unwittingly predicted his own future when he earlier renounced as sour grapes his dream of happiness through marriage with Sally. "All marriages ended the same. After five years—bickering, little affairs on the side, a resentful tolerance, no more desire." He achieves that end almost immediately. His last small vision of possible small happiness is the short paragraph that concludes the novel: "Norman poured himself a stiffer drink. He wondered whether Vivian would object to asking Kate round to dinner tomorrow night." Kate is Vivian's beautiful cousin.

It is a grim ending, underscored by the fact that Ernst ends up in much the same matrimonial boat. In Canada chance offers him the opportunity to save an old Jew from the prematurely falling wall of a building that is being demolished. Even better, he almost loses his own life in the process. Buried and nearly dead beneath the rubble, Ernst is finally happy, for some kind of balance has been reestablished. Then, although a hero to the League for Jewish Gentile Friendship, he is summarily claimed by Frau Kramer, "a tall, bony, severe" middle-aged German widow who is also "vehemently proud of the fact that her late father had served in the S.S." Ernst, in traction in his hospital bed, "despairingly" submits to her kisses, to her public proclamation that he is her fiancé. He dislikes her, he is afraid of her, but she has something on him. He is using her dead husband's identification papers, papers that he purchased from her. So Ernst goes even more reluctantly

than Norman into a darker marriage. Both find,
then, a separate peace at the end of *A Choice of
Enemies,* but in neither case is that peace better
than the war that came before. It is a grim vision,
but it is subtly and effectively sustained in a
work that must be seen as Richler's first major
novel.

5

~~~~~~~~~~~~~~~~~~~~~~~~~~~~~~~~

The Adventures of a *Pusherke* in *The Apprenticeship of Duddy Kravitz*

Richler's next novel, The Apprenticeship of Duddy Kravitz, is, unquestionably, one of his masterpieces. In this book he portrays a protagonist typically ridiculed in literature. Duddy Kravitz is the *pusherke*, the "pushy Jew," who, as several other characters in the work observe, almost gives anti-Semitism a good name. In Richler's hands, however, the *pusherke* is humanized and understood. He is assessed within the context of his immediate Jewish neighborhood; within the larger context of post–World War II Montreal; within the still larger context of modern North America. In each setting Duddy is a survivor, a swindler with a heart not of gold but of brass. Richler neither castigates nor exonerates Duddy. He neither sentimentalizes nor romanticizes. Instead, Duddy is dispassionately assessed. Through that authorial dispassion Richler also examines the hypocrisies of many (Gentiles and Jews) more honest and honorable than Duddy. But most of all, Duddy Kravitz represents a new twist to the Horatio Alger fable:

now the bad boy makes good. In effect, Richler rewrites the American Dream, casting in the hero's role a crude, calculating, callow, ill-mannered, and occasionally inept young Jew from St. Urbain Street.

Much of Richler's success with the character—and characterization—of Duddy derives from his remarkably skillful use of shifting points of view. As seen in the earlier novels, and especially in *A Choice of Enemies*, one of the hallmarks of Richler's technique is a careful control of narrative distance. Such control is even more obvious in *The Apprenticeship of Duddy Kravitz*. We see Duddy as he sees himself and as others see him; we view him triumphant within the small world of Fletcher's Field High School and totally humiliated (a humiliation that will change to triumph) in the world of affluent, sophisticated Jews whom he meets at Rubin's summer resort hotel, a kind of Grossinger's of the Laurentians. By turns *schlemiel* and swindler, a waiter turned boy-tycoon who soon goes bankrupt only to rise again, Duddy is certainly one of the most original of Richler's characters. Although he can be totally immoral (and Richler avoids the cliché of pleading the higher virtues of amorality), Duddy is still so vitally, so innocently committed to his own view of his own good that it is hard to condemn him out of hand. One critic, Warren Tallman, has even found in Duddy a hero for our times, a truly modern man whose frenetic scheming reflects the "accelerated image" that his age demands. Tallman praises Duddy for the honesty of his appetites, for his exuberance; in contrast, A. R. Bevans sees this same protagonist as a human disaster who, far from achieving any real success, "destroyed himself and . . . those who loved him."[1] In short, it is hard to get a "fix" on Duddy. Which is precisely Richler's point: the stereotype, the despised *pusherke*, has his own story to tell, but, as Duddy laments: "Nobody's ever interested in my side of the story." Richler is.

And a good story it is. The novel opens with Duddy, a senior at Fletcher's Field High, leading a gang of hooligans in escapades that verge on the malicious. Soon Duddy's attention centers on John MacPherson, an elderly teacher whose failed dreams (he was once an idealistic socialist) and flagging self-esteem have been reduced to one principle, his refusal to "strap a boy." An alcoholic and married to an invalid, MacPherson is patiently enduring the final years of employment that will entitle him to a pension; he is also less overtly waiting for liberation from a life as nursemaid to the wife he once, he remembers, loved. MacPherson runs afoul of Duddy Kravitz when he demands that the student get rid of a cigarette. Duddy insists that his father condones the smoking; the teacher counters: "Then he's not fit to bring up a boy." He realizes his mistake as soon as the words have been spoken. As soon as he has turned away, he feels the plunk of a snowball on the back of his neck. Yet despite the ensuing escalation of offenses, MacPherson will not, at first, stoop to strapping Duddy: "That he no longer believed in not strapping was beside the point. As long as he refused to do it Mr.

MacPherson felt that he would . . . survive." But, plagued by such pranks as late-night anonymous phone calls, the teacher is soon brought to the point where he straps often and happily. He does not survive; more accurately, his invalid wife does not. Returning late from a party, he finds that she has left her bed to answer the phone and collapsed on the floor. When she subsequently dies, MacPherson pointedly accuses Duddy of murder. Duddy denies having made the call, but we later find that he did. We also find that, much later, he can still feel guilty because of that act.

The opening section of the novel documents the breaking of MacPherson, who does crack up and has to be institutionalized. But the opening scenes also set up important thematic foci for the rest of the book. First, we see that Duddy can be ruthless when challenged. He is thin-skinned and quick to take offense, slow to forgive. Second, Duddy has a killer instinct. He goes for the jugular and always seems to know, almost intuitively, what someone's weakest point will be. At the same time, the high school misadventure attests to two of Duddy's more admirable attributes. He is not so dumb as he seems—as he seems especially to his own family. And more important, he is passionately, fiercely devoted to his family. Continually he disrupts his career as boy-tycoon in order to come to the rescue of family members who think he is nothing but a dismissable kid. His triumph, and his tragedy, is that his final, material success equally endears him to and alienates him from the family from which he was half-alienated all along. All that he achieves is the reversal of the half-alienation. His beloved and loving grandfather finally rejects him. His father, who had persistently favored the older brother, Lennie, turns to Duddy and makes him a new main character in the strained stories of "great men I have known" that allow Max Kravitz to hold up his head a little higher among his fellow taxi drivers and the prostitutes for whom he pimps.

Richler's versatile narrative perspective comes into play early in the novel. The first ten short chapters of Part One show Duddy triumphant within the grubby confines of the classroom, the schoolyard, and the street. The last four chapters show him to be a dupe and a fool, an uncertain, overeager, and naive schoolboy trying to survive among older and more sophisticated McGill college students who complacently anticipate their already assured futures. The very qualities that served Duddy at Fletcher's Field High make him a joke to the McGill set and particularly to Irwin Shubert, one of the older students working at Rubin's resort hotel for the summer. Just as Duddy had persecuted MacPherson, now Irwin taunts and torments Duddy, because Duddy embodies the "ghetto mentality" that Irwin thinks he has fled.

But Richler, in this section of the novel, does not take satisfaction in providing the protagonist with his "just desserts." On the contrary, he shows that Duddy is not as bad as he first seemed to be. The episode at Rubin's serves, in a sense, to elicit our sympathy for the same character whom we were invited to condemn in the first chapters of the novel. Unless he pushes, he is pushed. His aggressiveness, then, is merely a survival mechanism, a necessary attribute of someone who does not reap the benefits of a rich uncle, a good address, or a university scholarship. The misadventures at Rubin's also show Duddy's vulnerabilities—his pathetic desire to be liked, to "be somebody." His aggressiveness parallels his insecurity.

One prank perpetrated on Duddy during the humiliating summer especially provides the impetus for his determination to rise in the world and his pilgrim's progress toward an earthly kingdom of riches. Irwin, with the assistance of his girlfriend, Linda Rubin, the proprietor's daughter, plans to dupe Duddy. Linda—sophisticated, beautiful, fast—suddenly seems to take an unlikely interest in the short, skinny, seventeen-year-old Duddy, who is egotistical enough not to be suspicious. First plied with drink and then "seduced" into promising to be the bank for a midnight game of roulette, the prospective victim is easily set up. The game will be played with Irwin's wheel but with Duddy's money, the three hundred dollars that he has earned during a summer of slavish endeavor. Duddy has been promised that he cannot lose; he has promised his one confidant (Yvette?) at the hotel that, if his growing apprehensions prove true and he is taken, he will simply drown himself. He loses, disappears into the night, and is pronounced dead by the hotel guests. Rubin is frantic that any hint of scandal will mean a loss of business. The men who won money from the pathetic youngster all feel responsible for his fate. When Duddy returns to the hotel the next morning, he is welcomed as a hero. Irwin returns the three hundred dollars that Duddy had lost. The hotel guests take up a collection and provide some five hundred dollars more. Duddy has acquired the "stake" he was after. Pride goeth before a rise; the boy is on his way. And he is on his way very much because of offended pride, as is shown by his next encounter with Linda:

"You think I'm dirt," he said, "don't you?"
Look at me, he thought, take a good look because maybe I'm dirt now.... But you listen here, kiddo. It's not always going to be like this. If you want to bet on something bet on me. I'm going to be a somebody and that's for sure.

His way, his apprenticeship, is not solitary. On his journey from innocence to ruthlessness—a journey that has its twists and turns—he is accompanied by Yvette, a pretty, young French Canadian woman who, while a chambermaid at Rubin's, quickly decides that she is fond of Duddy. Like him, she is from a poor family. Being poor, she can partly share his dream, his instantaneously conceived "plan" to buy all the land surrounding the pristine lake to which she once takes him on a picnic. She even becomes the secret and not-so-secret accomplice without whose assistance he could never have succeeded. So Duddy's treatment of Yvette becomes another touchstone whereby we can judge him during the course of his material rise. In this case he is found wanting. From the beginning, Yvette is no more than a convenience, an object. He shows her as little consideration as Linda showed him.

Yvette's low status is exemplified both comically and pathetically the second time they make love. She has dressed in her best and prepared a delicious lunch for the special lake-shore outing she has planned. Dessert will begin with a session of skinny dipping in the secluded lake. But Duddy, who has often been preoc-cupied with thoughts of sex—he recommends *God's Little Acre* to practically everyone he meets—finds himself much more interested in the lake than in the naked girl who was about to enter it with him. He "hardly noticed" her un-dressing. He "broke rudely free of her embrace" to race to the lake, there to dive and sport with a suddenly dawning dream of the future. The romantic hideaway will become another Jewish holiday resort, bigger and gaudier than even Rubin's. His only concern is that someone else might horn in, so he tries to buy Yvette's silence regarding the lake, an offer that deeply offends her. When that fifty-dollar misunderstanding is resolved and the two finally make love, Duddy is still prefunctory, preoccupied. As George Wood-cock has observed, the whole scene is Chek-hovian in execution, a finely rendered exercise in noncommunication between characters who, even at their most intimate, talk mostly to themselves in an unharmonious duet.[2]

Duddy made love quickly to Yvette by the shore. "I feel so good," she said. "Do you feel good?"

He could watch the lake over her shoulder and in his mind's eye it was not only already his but the children's camp and the hotel were already going up. On the far side there was a farm reserved for his grandfather.

"I've never felt better."

"Do you like me? A little, even."

"Sure. Sure thing."

. . . Yvette lit a cigarette for him and Duddy decided where he would put the camp play field. The land there is as flat as a pool table, he thought. It's a natural. His heart began to pound again and he laughed happier than he had ever laughed before.

It is a happiness that excludes the woman with whom he has just made love, the woman who showed him the lake.

Despite this inauspicious beginning, Yvette still becomes Duddy's Girl Friday. She cooks for him, types for him, sleeps with him. Soon, as he strives to rise in the world, she functions as an unpaid secretary/manager, overseeing his tangled business commitments. And all along, because she is of legal age and French, she buys, in her own name, the coveted land from the French landholders and signs all of the necessary documents. And all along she is treated with the same friendly contempt:

Yvette wanted to wait, but Duddy insisted, and they made love on the carpet.

"I don't get it," Duddy said. "Imagine guys getting married and tying themselves down to one single broad for a whole lifetime when there's just so much stuff around."

"People fall in love," Yvette said. "It happens."

"Planes crash too," Duddy said. "Listen, I've got an important letter to write. We'll eat soon. O.K.?"

She didn't answer and Duddy began to type.

The reader well might wish that Yvette were more ruthless, that she would do what she once threatens and walk off with the deed to Duddy's precious land, leaving him, once more, out in the cold. But Duddy does not worry about the threat the few times it is voiced: "What is this? Traitor's night on Tupper Street? I'm hungry. Make dinner." Nor does he have to; Richler writes satirical fiction, not a morality play; the Yvettes of the world seldom leave the Duddys in the lurch—even when they should.

Yet Yvette is more than another demonstration of Richler's self-confessed propensity to portray women as one-dimensional figures.[3] Yvette, of course, has been seen as a definitely flat character. She is "little more than a conscience figure or a moral idea."[4] "On Yvette's side, the motivation is simple and stereotyped: her nature is to give rather than to take. Duddy is all skin and bones and needs mothering, she will stay with him until she finds someone else who needs mothering more than he does."[5] Her role, however, is more complicated. She is accomplice and conscience, muse and foil. These odd conjunctions are still more odd in that we never really see what she gains from the conflicting capacities in which she acts. Part of the problem is that Richler posits her love as a "given" in the novel, just as Duddy accepts it, unquestioningly, as such. When Peter Friar, Duddy's partner in moviemaking, asks him how he can trust Yvette, he says, matter-of-factly, "you have to trust somebody in this world." That sentiment, however, does not keep Duddy from continually betraying her trust.

Nevertheless, she not only helps him toward his goal, she actively pursues it with him and for him, calling notaries, checking out properties, making promises to buy when there is no money with which to buy, bargaining, wheeling and dealing. We never see the plot from her point of view, so we cannot understand her motivations. But apparently she too enjoys playing at being a real estate baron. Buying up the land owned by wealthier French Canadians also allows her a certain pride and status that, as a chambermaid, she certainly did not possess. So it is curious that, although Yvette subtly leads Duddy on, cooperating in the land-acquisition venture, emphasizing his first partial success and pointing out how close he is to final success, she is also shocked by the means he uses. As David Myers observes, Yvette, the "shrewd businesswoman," coexists rather uneasily with Yvette, the "lily-pure conscience constantly chiding the hapless Duddy."[6] The point seems to be that Yvette participates in Duddy's vision but does not fully share it. In some ways, the goal of owning the lake is, for her, a romantic fantasy, almost a game. For Duddy the same goal becomes an obsession, a key to his own identity, the cure to his insecurities.

Yvette serves a second function in the novel, one that she shares with Simcha Kravitz,

Duddy's grandfather. Simcha, the beloved *Zeyda*, and Yvette are the only two characters who appreciate Duddy, who see his best qualities and also understand his weaknesses. Also, it is Simcha who early in the novel provides the seven-year-old Duddy with the dicta that will become the boy's ruling passion: "A man without land is a nobody. Remember that, Duddel." The grandfather's own activity, perennially harvesting inedible vegetables from "the gritty hostile soil of his backyard," lends conviction to the assertion. Duddy is determined that the grandfather should finally have a real farm on the shores of the lake that Duddy will own. Ironically, Duddy works, schemes, lies, and cheats to fulfill the fantasies largely supplied by the only two people who love him, Yvette and Simcha. Ironically, by realizing their fantasies, he also undermines their faith in him and destroys their love. In short, he fulfills their fantasies by betraying their ideals.

Can ideals coexist, the novel asks, with fantasies that necessarily run counter to those very ideals? This question particularly applies to Simcha and Yvette. How different is Simcha's vision of ownership from Duddy's? But the same question also has a larger and more general application. Whether it is labeled the American Dream, the Canadian Dream, or the Jewish Dream, Simcha and Yvette still envision their own version of the dream that drives Duddy, the same old dream of liberation through ownership, of mystical fulfillment through essentially material means. Jay Gatsby learned in 1922 that

that equation does not work. Richler, in 1959, shows why it cannot, how the dream is always premised on a split in reality and a confusion of ends and means. The pursuit of the dream, by whatever means necessary, is justified by the dream. In contrast, one who fails to pursue a cherished dream is proved a failure by the unfulfilled dream. Duddy is, from one point of view (if one assesses the end achieved), a successful Simcha. From another perspective (if we examine the way to that end), he is, of course, a failed Simcha. In short, the dream itself has its own dark underside.

If we do not see this underside so clearly in the case of Duddy, we do with Dingleman, the Boy Wonder whom Duddy's father so much admires and who early in Duddy's life provides him with the model of what he would like to become. "He liked to think . . . that point for point he was a lot like the Boy Wonder before he had made his name." Duddy dreams in this fashion even after it is clear what Dingleman has become:

At thirty he was no longer a handsome man. His shoulders and chest developed enormously and his legs dwindled to thin bony sticks. He put on lots of weight. Everywhere he went the Boy Wonder huffed and puffed and had to wipe the sweat from the back of his rolled hairy neck with a handkerchief.

As with other such characters in the Richler canon, particularly the Star Maker of *Cocksure*, physical abnormalities symbolize a spiritual and emotional ugliness. And neither is the Dingleman Duddy actually encounters the wondrous

Boy Wonder of Max Kravitz's barroom yarns. He is a thoroughly corrupt man who dupes Duddy—"The boy is innocent. He's perfect" —into accompanying him to New York, in order to send him home with a coffee can filled with heroine. If Duddy were caught, he would clearly be stuck with the punishment for the smuggling that he does not even know he is committing. Still later, Dingleman would happily swindle Duddy out of all the lake front land that he has already acquired. Duddy is small potatoes when compared to a real conniver. Yet the parallels remain, and one Boy Wonder might be merely following in the crooked footsteps of another.

A second paradigm of success and of the failure of success is set forth by Mr. Cohen, a character who several times half-comes to Duddy's financial rescue. Cohen organizes the collection at Rubin's after the roulette fiasco. Later Duddy cons Cohen into allowing him to make (and to make a considerable profit on) *Happy Bar-Mitzvah, Bernie!* a monumentally bad avant-garde movie of a son's coming of age. Besides providing the comic pinnacle of the novel, the bar-mitzvah espisode also reveals how the "haves" like Mr. Cohen are as insecure as the "have nots" like Duddy Kravitz. Still later, when Duddy is at his lowest, Cohen offers advice and a substantial loan. His generosity is prompted by his recognition of Duddy as a younger version of himself. Indeed, his advice on how to be tough —the account of the "swindles" and "diddles" that keep him from "going under," the story of the *goy* who died slowly, crushed beneath a defective derrick in Cohen's junkyard, and how the health inspector and the coroner had to be bought off—amount to an apology for his own life and way of life. Duddy, by implication, will also have to cheat and steal in order to prosper; in order, possibly, to provide for his children so that they can become doctors or lawyers, for example, instead of working beneath "faulty derricks for thirty-five bucks a week." Once again Richler juxtaposes the "pure" dream of the fantasy end and the less than pure means, the often twisted roads to riches that are not examined in most of our parables of success.

In the first scenes of the novel we saw Duddy pushing and bragging his way to such small triumphs as being president of Room 41 at Fletcher's Field High. In the second sequence he is awed by the rich at the summer resort. He would be like them, but he must first learn to see them for what they are. His originally skewed vision is perfectly represented by the description of his preparation for the "date" with Linda—the protagonist attempting to "pass":

Duddy took half an hour combing his hair into a pompadour with the help of lots of brilliantine. He selected from among his shirts a new one with red and black checks and the tie he chose was white with a black and blue pattern of golf balls and clubs. His green sports jacket had wide shoulders, a one-button roll, and brown checks. A crease had been sewn into his grey flannel trousers. He wore two-tone shoes.

Later he "sees" less ludicrously and, modeling himself more on Cohen than on Dingleman, pushes and connives his way to successes more substantial than those achieved at Fletcher's or envisioned at Rubin's. "You'll go far, Kravitz. You're going to go very far," MacPherson had predicted, at the conclusion of his unfortunate altercation with Duddy. He was not completely wrong and neither was he, in the ironic sense he intended, completely right.

The Apprenticeship of Duddy Kravitz is, in several ways, *The Great Gatsby* without Daisy —and without the moral temporizing that Daisy and the "Dream of Love" supply, perhaps speciously, to that earlier novel of material success achieved by less noble means. Duddy is no hero, and *that* is the point. Until the end of the novel he continues to embody the contradictions we saw almost immediately. He can live persistently in Lennie's shadow, resent the ways in which his father and his Uncle Bernie both blatantly favor the older brother, yet he is the one who saves Lennie's botched medical career, and does so in a fashion that also saves the illusions of his father and his uncle. He can be kind, considerate to his family, yet he will shrewdly and viciously pursue his own objectives. A capable calculator, he is also naive, vulnerable, and, at times, extremely gullible. There is a larger point regarding the gullibility. It is unclear—and probably deliberately ambiguous—whether Richler wants us to view Duddy's naiveté as a flaw continually impeding him in his way toward wealth, or whether it is his saving grace, a redeeming quality in a character otherwise dedicated only to greed and connivance.

Flaw or saving grace, Duddy's naiveté does make for his one major crisis of conscience in the novel, and, whether we approve of him or not, this crisis does require that we once more at least sympathize with Duddy. Again we have one of Richler's calculated shifts in perspective, a ploy that regularly requires a reassessment of the novel's protagonist. Just as the tough young juvenile delinquent of Fletcher's Field could become the vulnerable young fool of Rubin's summer resort, so too can Duddy, the young man on the make and one who has almost made it, suddenly metamorphose into a sensitive soul wracked by a guilty conscience. The *pusherke* becomes almost a holy saint, and in the process he loses his shirt. Handled by a less skillful writer, this dark night of the soul would strain credibility. But, because Duddy's insecurities and even his tenderness have always been there, the reader is not unduly surprised when another side of Duddy suddenly surfaces and briefly dominates his conscious concerns.

The cause of his crisis of conscience is the accident involving Virgil, an epileptic would-be poet who adores Duddy because Duddy gave him a job. The irony is that Duddy's kindness to Virgil was not prompted by any inklings of decency. Far from it—Duddy hires the handicapped driver in order not to pay him the thousand dollars he owes him for the contraband pinball machines that Virgil has smuggled into Canada. Duddy profits from the pinball machines and profits again when he has Virgil drive the truck for his film distribution and rental business. So here again we face the problem of perspective. Duddy connives, yet Virgil worships him because of the "opportunity" connivance provided. The same double perspective also emphasizes the previously discussed duplicity of Yvette. She retrospectively and most explicitly condemns Duddy for permitting an epileptic to drive. But, if Yvette violently objected to Virgil driving, why did she not intercede before the crash? Once more she acts as conscience, but a conscience after the fact, a consideration that calls the judgment of that conscience into question.

Nevertheless, Virgil's accident and Yvette's subsequent withdrawal throw Duddy into a mental and spiritual tailspin. The accident also revives, for Duddy, the earlier fate of MacPherson and his wife. In order to cope with massive guilt, he engages in classic self-punishment. He does not eat or sleep; he almost deliberately offends all of his most important clients; he fails to keep appointments. In a matter of days, Duddy is forced to the edge of bankruptcy and barely stirs from his self-destructive lethargy to recognize the fact that he is ruined. He seems to suspect (perhaps only subconsciously) that a Duddy without money is the symbolic equivalent of a Virgil Roseboro without legs or a Jenny MacPherson without life. Clearly, the financial collapse is a kind of offering to the gods—to Yvette, to Virgil, to the MacPhersons, to whatever fates govern lives. His passionate withdrawal from the path to success signals the depth of his sensitivity. All past evidence to the contrary, Duddy is human after all.[7] And once the reader is reassured of that fact, Richler can get on with the real story—Duddy's rise to riches.

Reunited with Virgil and Yvette, Duddy quickly forgets his former pain. Once more, and once more at Yvette's initiative, he is in pursuit of land. But after near bankruptcy, success is much harder to come by, and Duddy is more and more driven beyond the edge of bare decency and acceptable sharp business practices. When one final plot of land must be quickly acquired, Duddy first attempts to coerce Virgil into putting up money (Virgil has a small inheritance) that he has promised Yvette he will not lend (Yvette knows Duddy). Then, when Virgil succumbs to another severe attack of epilepsy, Duddy forges one of Virgil's checks. He steals outright, and from a sick friend, in order to possess his dream. Half-realizing how much he has transgressed, Duddy quickly arranges for Yvette to sign over the rest of the land, lest she decide to punish him by keeping the property that is legally still in her name. She signs, and the whole lake is finally his. He has accomplished his dream.

The ending of the novel balances on the final downward tilting of the moral scale. Even Duddy's fall, his worst act, is presented through the polarity of two quite-different perspectives. He would view the not-quite-authentic thousand-dollar check as an aberrant means to an end so manifestly just that it must redeem the means. At the worst, "in [his] desperate condition," he has succumbed only to irregular borrowing, for he insists that he will repay Virgil later. "With another truck?" Yvette might have asked. She sees the forged signature and the fact that Duddy has now robbed the man he had already crippled.

A similar balance pervades the final episode of the novel. The Kravitz family's country excursion arranged by Duddy will finally show Lennie, Max, and Simcha (brother, father, and grandfather) the fruits of Duddy's labors. When they arrive at the lake, they discover they are not alone. There, too, are Linda and the Boy Wonder. So Duddy has the pleasure of kicking them both off his property. With the erstwhile Golden Girl, Duddy clearly wins the unvoiced bet that he made after she tricked him into being the dupe of the roulette prank. He is already "somebody" (and she has already begun to play up to him); now she—Dingleman's current kept woman—is dirt in his eyes. The Boy Wonder, who earlier profited from Duddy's naiveté and who tried to scheme the lake away from Duddy, also slinks off into the setting sun, vanquished by a younger version of himself: " 'On my land,' [Duddy] shouted, 'no trespassers and no cripples,' " as he brandished a stone at his retreating rival.

Duddy triumphs over Linda and the Boy Wonder, yet fails miserably with those who loved him most. To start with, on discovering the forgery, Virgil has another fit. Yvette tells Duddy to phone for an ambulance; Duddy, however, rushes out of the room in a blind panic, afraid that he will fall again into the despair that had earlier claimed him. "Duddy ran, he ran, he ran." But he cannot run far enough and is soon caught once more, this time by Simcha. At the height of Duddy's triumph, the *Zeyda* both negates his dream and denies the dreamer. Simcha will not accept the farm that Duddy offers; he will not even admire the new property. The grandfather, characterized throughout the novel as a man of principles, knows what the lake has cost in personal morality. Yvette has told Simcha about Virgil, about why and how he was crippled, about how and when he was cheated, and about Duddy's callousness and his dishonesty, qualities that Simcha despises. Simcha also sees through Duddy's promised generosity: " 'I can see what you have planned for me, Duddel. You'll be good to me. You'd give me everything I wanted. And that would settle your conscience when you went out to swindle others.' "

Simcha is right, and Duddy knows it. His only defense is to lash out even at the beloved *Zeyda:* "A man without land is nothing. That's what you always told me. Well, I'm somebody. A real somebody. . . . You couldn't even go to see Uncle Benjy before he died. Naw, not you. You're just too goddam proud to live. You—" Duddy breaks off the accusations and tries to turn them into an apology, but the *Zeyda* will not look at him, and later Lennie reports that the old man is crying. Is this the price of success? Is success worth the price?

Richler suggests that it is, and it isn't. Even the last sentences of the novel both affirm and deny Duddy's vision, as well as Simcha's and Yvette's ideals. Max, Duddy's father, waiting for Duddy in a restaurant, is regaling strangers with

stories of how a nervy kid made good. They are
the same stories that he has always told, except
Duddy has now replaced the Boy Wonder as the
subject of Max's compensatory fables. Duddy,
who has just come from his final—and it will be
the final—meeting with Yvette, is angry at what
he hears. He cannot buy the father's story,
because he has just experienced, firsthand, the
lie behind the myth of the self-made man: " 'In a
minute!' Duddy said, 'I'm going to explode. I'm
going to hit somebody so hard—' " Yet he cannot
sustain his self-hatred either. Even as he is asking his father to pick up the tab— "Em, I haven't
any cash on me. Daddy, can you . . . ?"—a waiter
steps forward and says he can sign the bill.
Duddy *is* recognized. He is a somebody. He has
made it:

And suddenly Duddy did smile. He laughed. He
grabbed Max, hugged him, and spun him around.
"You see," he said, his voice filled with marvel. "You
see."

It is the marvel, the laughter, the innocent
hugging of his foolish father that redeem Duddy
and the novel. Neither a criticism of the *pusherke*
in the mode of *What Makes Sammy Run?* nor a
Horatio Alger celebration of the success ethic,
The Apprenticeship of Duddy Kravitz is about,
simply, apprenticeship. Duddy's status is still
uncertain at the end of that apprenticeship. He is
a success; he owns the land; Lou's Bagel and Lox
Bar will extend him credit. And he is still penni-
less, with a hotel still to be built and land to be

developed. But Duddy is only twenty years old and quite undaunted. At forty he would probably not possess the sense of wonder of the apprentice. That, however, is another novel. But the moral of that other novel, suggested in this one by Cohen and even more by the Boy Wonder, hangs ominously over the ending, a hint of nightmare in Duddy's realized dream.

6

The Incomparable Atuk:
A Canadian Eskimo's
American Dream

The title of The Incomparable Atuk suggests a
certain satiric borrowing from *The Great Gatsby.*
Gatsby may have been "great," but Atuk is
"incomparable." The similarity between the two
works extends considerably beyond their titles,
however, for Atuk pursues his dream of his own
destiny with a dedication worthy of Gatsby
himself. Atuk, moreover, has much the same
obstacles in his way as had Jay Gatsby. The Canadian Arctic is even more provincial (in the
pejorative sense), more remote from any center
of civilization, than is the American Midwest.
Nonetheless, Atuk, a Baffin Bay Eskimo, leaves
the scene of his humble beginnings to rise to
some fame and fortune in his country's cultural
capital. He goes south to Toronto, first to be a
poet and then to pursue the more lucrative trade
of entrepreneur. Atuk also pursues his unex-
amined dream of success to essentially the same
end that Gatsby achieved. The novel ends with
Atuk certain that he will make a killing in a
rigged quiz show with a most unusual gimmick.
Strapped in a guillotine, he plays "Stick Out
Your Neck"—a "million bucks" if he wins and

"KER-PLUNK!" if he loses. Of course Atuk loses, loses to die a death more meaningless and more grotesque than Gatsby's murder in his swimming pool.

These comic parallels to and mock inversions of *The Great Gatsby* bring us to the heart of Richler's novel. *The Incomparable Atuk*, a "Canadianized" version of the American novel, is something more than the slight topical satire that its few critics have postulated.[1] The book, in its way, is a devastating critique of both the "American Dream" of materialistic success and the "Americanizing" of Canada. The "American Dream" becomes the "Canadian Dream"; the "Canadian Dream" becomes the "Eskimo Dream." Atuk's—by the time it reaches him—thirdhand dream brings that would-be poet from Baffin Bay in the Arctic north to seek his fortune in the more promising climes of Toronto to the south. The dream also brings Atuk to seek his fortune in a field more financially rewarding than poetry. Inspired by Dr. Burt Parks, a Canadian proponent of the power of positive thinking—Parks's phrase, "What you dare to dream; dare to do," runs like a refrain through the novel—and by a chance observation of the prices charged for Eskimo sculpture by Toronto art shops, Atuk abandons poetry to found "Esky Enterprises." He brings south all but the most incorrigibly lazy members of his family and gets them to turning out deliberately crude Eskimo paintings and statues. Since he pays his workers only with cheap baubles and the privilege of watching TV (a privilege cancelled if production figures fall off), the profits roll in. The young man is on his way.

A crude and exploitative commercialism pervades the novel and underlies even such unlikely events as the original discovery of Atuk as a poet. The Eskimo became nationally known when his poems "ran in a series of advertisements in magazines all across Canada." Those advertisements were underwritten by The Twentyman Fur Company, a "vastly misunderstood enterprise" being criticized at the time "in press and parliament." The cause of the publicity was the Eskimo's plight—"dying of consumption, malnutrition, and even frost-bite, all because of what the white man [and more specifically the fur traders] had done to make his [the Eskimo's] accustomed way of life unfeasible." To rectify this problem—the fur company's problem, not the Eskimo's—a Twentyman adman sent north to polish up the image of the company barters with Atuk and, in exchange for a "sheaf" of "verses," provides the native with a cigarette lighter and two electric blankets (sure cure for frostbite), a sack of flour and a dozen chocolate bars (to stave off malnutrition). Ads containing Atuk's poems appear in the national magazines. All Canada can see that fur companies do not reduce the Eskimos to poverty but raise them to poetry.

From the beginning, then, Atuk is the creature of Buck Twentyman, the ultimate tycoon and the villain of the novel. He becomes, for example, an established poet not so much because he is talented but because Twentyman requires his talent, such as it is. It is not much either. His "best loved poem, the one that had appeared in ... the national advertisements," reads:

> I go hunt bear in white dawn,
> good spirit come with me.
> I go fish in silver twilight,
> good spirit come with me.
> Over the white crust soon comes
> forever night
> good spirit,
> O, spirit,
> stay with me.

Atuk can publicly warble these Arctic-night notes wild because Twentyman Fur Company wants a singing Eskimo commercial: "Look how happy our darkies are!" So the poet is later pointedly castigated when he once replaces his "arctic simplicity" with borrowed beat and sings a different song:

> Twentyman Fur Company,
>   I have seen the best seal hunters of my
> generation putrefy raving die from tuberculosis,
>   Massey, you square,
> eskimos don't rub noses any more and the cats
>   around Baffin Bay dig split-level houses.
>   Listen to me, Pearson,
>   a house is not a home,
>   an igloo is not a pad.
> And you, Diefenbaker, can kiss my ass
> where holy most holy pea-soup hockey players
>   have rumbled.

Canada, wake up, you're all immigrants to me:
my people are living like niggers.

This Eskimo *Howl* "took Twentyman's name in vain." Atuk is to clear all future poems with the Twentyman adman who discovered him.

Soon, Richler shows, Atuk has learned the lesson of his master and is playing the proper commercial game. Even in the john he will dictate a poem and, at the same time, calculate where and for how much he might be able to sell it:

"Atuk to Stainsby," he wrote, "poem, esk. style, broad. rights, CBC Anthology, pay, min. $100. Pub. rights, McAllister's Fort., min. pay, ditto."

And then the poem, bland as baby food and appropriate for the most undeveloped palates:

O plump and delicious one
here in land of so short night
me
alone,
humble,
hungering.

In Toronto, the Eskimo has learned how the world turns. His radio is on all night, tuned to a station that might give him "a free television set, washing machine or wristwatch with automatic calendar and built-in alarm," provided he is listening if the station calls. In the city of opportunity, "an alert Eskimo could even make a start on his fortune while he slept." Or while he strolls the streets: any place in the city, "Atuk zigzagged

in and out of the magic eye doors of the super-
markets, chain drugstores, and department
stores ... just in case he should be the One Mil-
lionth Happy Customer to pass through These
Friendly Doors, and therefore be showered with
munificence." It is at this point, too, that Atuk
imports sundry relatives to staff a "basement
factory" and begins to churn out true Canadian
folk art, Eskimo statues that tend to be only
slightly inferior to similar products imported
from Japan. Soon he is thinking on an even
larger level. No more "ignorant nieces breaking
up cigars to spice the stew"; no more "gluttonous
... uncles boiling his tooled leather belts in the
soup." There has to be, he muses, "another
answer. Moulds. Machinery. Mass production."

Richler's Eskimo is clearly no standard
Rousseauvian savage undone by the crass commercialism of a world that he never made. Yet
Atuk can play the part of the noble native if
occasion requires. Charged once by one of his
early patrons, Professor Gore, with selling out to
Twentyman, whose fur company "exploits your
people," Atuk responds: "Men with greased
words come here and ask me to sign little papers.
I am grateful for Toronto's goodness to me. They
give me money. I sign. I am able to send money
to the Bay to fight my people's hunger and sick-
ness. Is that bad, Professor?" His tone—the guile-
less innocent exploited by the city slicker—is
pure hokum. When it comes to promoting an
image, Atuk is at this point as innocent as a good
presidential press secretary. For example, when
a "lady in Regina" sends him a pair of "dreadful"

knitted socks, Atuk does not throw the present out: "Treated properly this was just the kind of heart-warming story that would make a big splash in the eastern papers. 'Develop,' Atuk wrote on top of the lady's letter, 'Hickvillewise.' " Nor is Atuk all that concerned with his people. When one brother who objected to Atuk's treatment of the family is out in the city for the first time, Atuk tells him how to cross the busy streets and get safely home: "You wait until [the traffic light is] red and then you run like hell."

One of Richler's most effective ironies is to create, in his Baffin Bay Eskimo, a protagonist who is ready to match the modern world before he ever encounters it. In fact, Atuk early demonstrated his capabilities as a competitor, a survivor. As a youth on the tundra, he once found it necessary to dine on a United States Intelligence Officer. The occasion of the meal is never described, so the extenuating circumstances, nationally pleaded when Atuk is finally apprehended, do not really extenuate. Yet the diner clearly feels no particular remorse regarding the demise and subsequent disappearance of one Colonel Swiggert. He had already learned his chief lesson in life and learned it well. His father, who, after a National Film Board short on Eskimo life, preferred to be called the Old One, "had taken" the son "on his lap and told him, 'For an Eskimo boy to make his mark in the world, Atuk, he must be brighter, better, and faster than other boys.' " And hungrier, it might be added.

It can also be noted that the Old One's paternal advice effectively emphasizes one of the main satiric thrusts in Richler's plot. The narrator goes on to observe that "Atuk had modelled his life on" the "precept" just quoted, and then shows how the son, during a typical day in Toronto, heeds his father's counsel: "So that morning he [Atuk] rose as usual at 6:30 a.m., ate a three-day-old crust of bread dipped in whale oil, washed it down with an ice-cold Pepsi and . . . set right down to work." In other words, Atuk can succeed in the modern world because he is himself a creature of that world, the stock character in an archetypal capitalist myth. Even from Baffin Bay, a young man on the make, convinced of the power of positive self-interest, can confidently set out to rise in the world.

Toronto—the world in which Atuk makes his rise—also provides Richler with numerous satiric targets. Atuk is at home in this city from the very beginning. Flown south to attend the publisher's party for his first book of poems, he encounters such treats as a striporama and a midget wrestling match and "simply refused to return to the Bay." He has seen the glitter and finds it good. That glitter is so much mined in the novel that one critic sees *The Incomparable Atuk* as "a satire on Canadian poses and pretenses so sharply localized that it is in fact a *roman a clef.*"[2] There are, admittedly, devastating parodies of particular people and especially those members of the Toronto literati who aspire to be, in a term from the novel, the "Tastemakers" of Canada. But we see posing and pretense of a more generic nature too: the would-be bohemian writer who flagrantly "shoots up" what is only the insulin he takes for diabetes; the good liberal professor so dedicated to the cause of social equality that he is mortally offended by, say, a flashily dressed black man (the objects of his concern have "no right" to treat his labors on their behalf in that disrespectful fashion); or, conversely, there is a Jewish businessman who "engaged only non-Jewish girls at the office [and hired German help at home] in order to demonstrate that he was utterly free of prejudice." On a still lower level of satire are the various characters in Dr. Parks' entourage, such as "the strongest stunted man in the world" or Bette Dolan, "Canada's Darling," the gullible young virgin whom Atuk so easily seduces and then abandons for someone fat, smelly, and somewhat more real. But on every level the essential element is the same. There is a claimed achievement, a claim of significance that simply is not justified. Dr. Parks himself sums up the whole matter perfectly when he observes that he is "world-famous . . . all over Canada."

The "farcical jungle of Canadian idiocies" that Richler charts in *The Incomparable Atuk* should not then, as George Woodcock suggests, detract from the story of Atuk.[3] Atuk, Eskimo that he is, is still a creature of that jungle. But more to the point, the jungle is an imitation jungle; it is mostly imported from the south. As I have already indicated, Richler's main target is double. Debased versions of an Americn dream pervade Canada as well as the United States. So the Canadian imitations, considering Canada's ineffec-

tual pretense at cultural independence and anti-
Americanism, are, for Richler, even more
ludicrous than the American originals. This judgment is implicit in the novel's epigraph:

What would happen in Canada if full sovereignty were
invoked and the southern border were sealed tight
against American mass culture—if the air-waves were
jammed, if all our comic books were embar-
goed, if only the purest and most uplifting of American cultural commodities were allowed entry. Native
industries would take over, obviously. Cut off from
American junk, Canada would have to produce her
own (Richard H. Rovere, *Macleans*, November 5,
1960).

Canadian junk would be produced, of course,
according to the familiar American models. But it
already is being produced that way. Atuk's first
paying job in Toronto is to write for *Metro, the
magazine for cool canucks*. The editor expounds
on the magazine's plight: "We're fighting for our
life here. We stand for a Canadian identity and
the American mags are trying to drive us out of
business." Then he gives Atuk his assignment. A
western story razored out of a 1940 issue of a
popular American magazine is to be "re-set . . . in
Moose Jaw 1850."

Yet Woodcock's criticism of the novel's lack
of focus is partly valid. The satire does sometimes get out of hand, and the targets can be
"topical in a rather ephemeral way."[4] The death
of little Wayne Peel, who, born sickly and un-
derweight, was treated with massive doses of
vitamins, "until, finally, too healthy to live he

died," really does not fit into the novel. The Peel family's regularly staged bomb-shelter drills, including the practice "execution" of a "neighbor" trying to take shelter in their shelter is definitely dated. Other episodes may only partly fit into the novel but they are so humorously managed that one can hardly object to their presence. Thus we have Sergeant Jock Wilson, "who decided to join the RCMP after he had seen Gary Cooper in *Northwest Mounted Police*"; who, later, in drag and as Jane, is assigned to seek subversives among the fast set; who (horrors!) falls in love with a young man being investigated, who (joy!) turns out to be a famous woman reporter disguised as a man and also investigating the fast set. Through a series of events too complex to summarize, Jock/Jane also ends up as Miss Canada and might even become Miss Universe, which would definitely be another "first for the force," but hardly in the envisioned Gary Cooper tradition. It is all amusing, and only the most uncompromising proponent of thematic unity could wonder whether the misadventures of Jock/Jane really complement those of Atuk.

Richler also does not resist the temptation to play satiric variations on a theme that he treated more seriously in his earlier fiction, and particularly in *Son of a Smaller Hero*. The Eskimo as outcast becomes the Eskimo as Jew. "We are the chosen pagans, my son," explains the Old One to Atuk. He also emphasizes that the chosen must stay chosen: "It all begins with taking a bath. It seems a little compromise, I know. But one day you take a bath and the next

you have turned your back on your own people."
The point of the warning is Atuk's plan to marry
one Goldie Panofsky. Her brother, Rory Peel, the
"liberated Jew" in the novel, opposes the match:

> "Atuk, I'm pleased to have you as a business
> associate. But you're not . . . well, fit to marry into a
> Jewish family."
> "You don't understand. Jewish, Protestant, you're
> all white to me."

The sardonic reversal is amusing, especially
when it is reversed again. "Being called white . . .
was the compliment, the state of grace, [Rory]
had striven for all his life." But voiced by Atuk,
that compliment becomes merely another racial
slur. Rory is now affronted that his own excluded
status is so cavalierly dismissed. All of which has
little to do with the main themes of the novel, but
it does show that Richler is as willing to satirize
Jewish matters as Canadian ones.

The sometimes wandering novel is thoroughly back on track in Part Three. Part One,
"What You Dare to Dream, Dare to Do," was
followed by Part Two, "Eskimo Tycoon." Both
lead to "This Was the Noblest Canadian of Them
All." As the title of Part Three—with its obvious
reference to the funeral of Julius Caesar—suggests, the wages of overweening ambition will be
death. That death comes when Atuk decides he is
more than a match for his mentor and former
model, Buck Twentyman, the preeminent
tycoon. The latter's rhetoric is Canadian, but his
interest is cash. To promote both his recently
acquired television station and a new line of

frozen foods, Esky-Foods, Twentyman comes up with a promising format for a quiz show and arranges for Atuk to be the first contestant. This show, "Stick Out Your Neck," epitomizes the chicanery and cupidity that motivate most of the characters in the book. It also serves to bring the novel full circle. *The Incomparable Atuk* begins with Twentyman importing a guillotine into Canada. It ends with Atuk in the guillotine, the guillotining, and Twentyman's wonderfully hypocritical funeral oration.

The show that was to be rigged so that Atuk would win was really rigged so that he would lose. Twentyman had earlier noted that he could profit more from a martyr than a hero. Besides, the real tycoon's Eskimo was getting uppity. Twentyman's newly formed company, Esky-Foods, was also "in direct competition with one of America's largest, most deeply entrenched . . . food combines." So Twentyman sells the sponsorship of "Stick Out Your Neck" to the American company, a fact he points out in the final sentences of the novel: " 'Atuk is dead.' He told them how, where, and pointed out the country of origin of the show's sponsor. 'Friends, Canucks, countrymen,' he went on, 'use your noggins . . .' " Twentyman here speaks to lament Atuk's passing to approximately the same degree that Mark Antony came to bury Caesar, not to praise him. Twentyman's message is really to buy Canadian, to buy Twentymanian. His fellow citizens should certainly not use their heads to wonder whether they should buy at all. Nor did Atuk use his. Quite the contrary; it was used. In several senses, Atuk was ripped off. Indeed, at the end of the novel, the basket of the guillotine contains the final demonstration of the high cost of his low dreams.

The Incomparable Atuk is, finally, a cutting satire on personal cupidity, pervasive commercialism, Canadian pretentions (Jewish, Gentile, and Eskimo), and, for Richler, the junk that passes, in Canada and the United States, as culture—both high culture and popular culture. A satire that takes on so many targets and does them in in so convincing a fashion surely merits some consideration.

7

~.~.~.~.~.~.~.~.~.~.~.~.~.~.~.~.~.~.

Popular Culture, Black Comedy, and *Cocksure*

Cocksure, *one of the author's favorites* among his novels, is also a pivotal book in the Richler canon.[1] Much more than the preceding novel, *The Incomparable Atuk*, it is the story of a Gentile who finds himself to be the "Jew" in an alien ghetto. One could even argue that *Cocksure* is Richler's most thorough treatment of the concept of "Jew," and that it is such a persuasive treatment precisely because Mortimer Griffin, the protagonist, is not technically a Jew. *Cocksure* is also the last novel in which Richler gives a major role to a personification of monstrous evil. The line of these super villains extends from Colonel Kraus in *The Acrobats* to the Star Maker in *Cocksure*. In *St. Urbain's Horseman*, however, Dr. Mengele is mostly off stage and out of the action, while Dr. Dr. Mueller in the recent *Joshua Then and Now* is, as the double Dr. might suggest, only a harmless fraud. But more important, *Cocksure* stands firmly (the pun is intended) between the sometimes sophomoric satire of *The Incomparable Atuk* and the mature social comedy of *St. Urbain's Horseman* and *Joshua Then and Now*. In short, *Cocksure* represents

Richler's most accomplished writing as a satirist; it is a devastating critique of those aspects of contemporary society that particularly offend the moral (and comic) sense of the author.

The setting of *Cocksure* is London in the sixties. The setting is also transplanted Hollywood, Hollywood transplanted as a kind of rank weed throughout the world. Again Richler attacks, on many different levels, the producers, directors, writers, and actors of merchandized fantasies that pervade the mass media. Mortimer Griffin, the WASP anti-hero of the novel, is a high-level editor of Oriole Press, a British-based publishing firm that is taken over by an "aging undying" movie mogul who suddenly, seemingly inexplicably, moves across the ocean to be closer to his British operations. This producer, Star Maker, turns out to be a grotesque emblem of fraudulent Hollywood, as well as fraudulent, "swinging" London. The epitome of self-concern, Star Maker aims first at self-perpetuation and then self-reproduction. When, in the first episode of the novel, the sycophantic Dino Tomasso, who has been designated as Star Maker's heir, finds that he is being demoted to the London operation, in one first and final burst of fury he tells Star Maker to "Go fuck yourself." This Star Maker decides to do. After a certain amount of surgical juggling, Star Maker finally consummates his relationship with himself in an act of autoeroticism that has obvious symbolic overtones for a society that is, increasingly, both narcissistic and hypersexual.

Mortimer comes to know more and more

about Star Maker's enterprises (on all levels) after he is chosen to be the new head of Oriole Publishing. He is chosen, incidentally, because of his "marvy lymphatic system." For those who work for Star Maker, however, good health is definitely unhealthy. Tomasso, for example, who had already contributed to Star Maker's well-being, is soon called upon to give more. First one eye and then the other are lost before this subordinate realizes how truly blind he has always been. Like Star Maker's other greedy lackeys, he has been willing to sacrifice—personal pleasures, moral principles, and body parts—all for the prospect of ultimately inheriting a piece of Star Maker's kingdom. But as Star Maker swells with child, Tomasso's hopes are dashed. He knows too much about the business. He must be replaced—and eliminated. Mortimer subsequently fares no better. The novel ends with the protagonist going the way of Tomasso. Mortimer, however, will be eliminated because of his refusal to abandon traditional values and his unwillingness to be a part of the murderous Star Maker industries.

As this summary should suggest, even on a satiric level, *Cocksure* is an impressive allegory of sin and damnation—and the wages of virtue. The novel operates on two other levels also. We see Mortimer within the domestic circle of his family and within the larger social circle of London life. In the bizarre, surrealistic world of Star Maker, Mortimer—the average, moral man—is dramatically out of place. But one of Richler's more subtle ironies is that Mortimer, a Canadian

WASP, is almost equally out of place within the "real" world of mod London. He is a square among the swingers, and the swingers run the show. In his own home, too, Mortimer seems always out of step.

His wife Joyce is, as much as he, a standard Canadian Protestant prude. But Joyce is determined to wear a public face of progressive liberalism. So she continually disparages her husband, describing even his "conventionally handsome" appearance with "unconcealed repugnance." Soon she leaves him for a more satisfying man. Mortimer's eight-year-old son also finds his father a trifle ridiculous. After Doug falls asleep, Mortimer can go into the boy's room, kiss his cheek, and ruffle his hair, something that he knows would be far too square for daylight hours. Unlike the father, the eight-year-old is never square. Doug calmly discusses with either parent the affair between his mother and the outrageous Ziggy Spicehandler. He also encourages the affair, keeping his father occupied and out of the house at the proper moments. It is eight-year-old Doug who advises Mortimer when the truth comes out: "I think you should cut out for a while and let them be. I'll come and stay with you on weekends, if you like. Maybe you could take me to Paris next weekend?" But after all, Doug has been, up to this point, the underprivileged product of an unbroken home. His parents had not competed with one another to buy his affection.

Mortimer's public life is disordered too. The focus of that disorder is provided by two contradictory accusations, Jacob Shalinsky's repeated charge, "You are a Jew," and I. M. Sinclair's countercharge, "You are an anti-Semite." Despite his best efforts to do so, Mortimer fails to defuse either accusation. Indeed, the two unresolved condemnations serve to tie together many strands of this novel. The question "What is a Jew?" becomes, in its more general form, "What is socially acceptable?" Or, conversely, depending on one's point of view, "What is not?" The moralistic implications of the satire are emphasized by the way in which Star Maker's grotesqueries are portrayed as more acceptable than traditional values such as honesty or fidelity or concern for family and fellow humans. So Sister Theresa, on Digby Jones's "Insult" show, is forced to admit that, as a virgin nun "not getting it regular" (her words translated into his idiom), she gets her jollies by ministering to the poor:

"Would it be altogether unfair, then, to describe you not as suppressed—*but as a sexually diverted nymphomaniac?* A pornographer of the do-good?"

As the unlying camera zoomed in on Sister Theresa's sobbing face, Dig demanded, "What is she, fans?"

"As shitty as we are!"

Yet Mortimer, until the very end, refuses to acknowledge that he is a Jew, déclassé in a society of hipsters. Throughout the novel he tries to play the games of those around him, usually with ludicrous results. For example, when Ziggy Spicehandler (né Gerald Spencer) telegrams to announce an impending visit, Mortimer instantly begins to unmake the order of his house. He jumbles all the books on his shelves, to avoid a disparaging "How tidy!" He disdains ownership by erasing his name from all his books. *Playboy* and *Evergreen Review* replace *The New Yorker* on the coffee table. "Doug's pissy old mattress" becomes the pièce de résistance in the yard that was recently a model of suburban neatness. After his frantic unmaking of his house, Mortimer rests, contented, and quite oblivious to the fact that he has merely moved from one form of meaningless conformism to another.

The sixties, so exuberantly extolled by the with-it characters in the novel, are no more free than were the repressive fifties. New rules are not no rules. They are also, sometimes, not even very different from the old rules, the evils of which they ostensibly correct. Thus, at a Beatrice Webb School parents' meeting, an "enlightened TV producer" who "deplored censorship" and the "Victorian double standards," can still think that "just because his thirteen-year-old daughter was the only girl in the fifth form to stop at petting . . . was no reason for her to come home with a scarlet *T* for 'tease' painted on her bosom."

New rules can also serve to confuse further the very issues that they are intended to resolve. This point is most convincingly made in a scene that effectively demonstrates how an au courant determination to be completely color-blind suspiciously resembles another generation's prejudice. The problem begins when Mortimer enters a bank one day and immediately notices a beautiful black woman standing in one line while elsewhere there are two free tellers. Might it not, Mortimer wonders, seem racist to refuse to take his place behind the black woman. That question is only a foretaste of more serious ones to come. Departing from the bank, the woman drops her glove. Now here is an insoluble dilemma. Is it racist to retrieve or not to retrieve the glove? If she is a radical black, he will be a patronizing "good-liberal" ofay if he stoops. If she is more traditional, he will be a callously blatant bigot if he does not. While Mortimer stands a victim of his doubts and indecisions, the woman picks up her own glove, whispers "mother fucker" under her breath, and leaves, leaving Mortimer, and the reader, to ponder the absurd irrelevance of his codes—all of them—to his encounter. The absurdity and irrelevance is only heightened when we later find out where all those twenty-five pound checks that the lady was cashing came from—an explanation that also explains the end to which she dropped the glove.

It is Mortimer's fate to be out of step with his time. Even his seeming virtues have become vices. "Yes, he had to admit, considering himself in the bathroom mirror, yes, yes, the sour truth is I'm tall and handsome.... Clean-cut, he might have added, unmistakably WASP, like the smiling sincere husband in the unit trust advertisements on whose forehead ran the slogan: 'Investor at 35, capitalist at 60.' " "Capitalist," of course, is the current term of contempt; WASP is the despised minority. But do what he will, Mortimer is unable to pass. At parties he is completely ignored. In bars, the "real" men clean up their stories as soon as Mortimer enters. He is, in effect, a male Miss Ryerson (his old grade school teacher), innately censorious, in best schoolmarm fashion, of all that smacks of any impropriety, despite his best efforts to be hip.

Shalinsky's false accusation has its ironic truth. Mortimer does not belong. Mortimer also does not see the advantages that well might accrue if he could only embrace the symbolic mode of nonbelonging/belonging that is offered to him and pass as a Jew by falsely confessing that he has previously attempted to pass as a Gentile. When the outs are in, it is in to be out. So Gerald Spencer, in tune with the times, can become "Ziggy Spicehandler"—and act as a Ziggy, not a Gerald. But Mortimer very much resents Shalinsky's persistent intimations of fraternity. Unlikely as it seems, he is what he most vociferously claims to be, a purebred WASP, a native of Caribou, Ontario, Canada. He also goes to considerable lengths to assert his authenticity, showing Shalinsky, for example, such documents as his birth certificate, as well as his "Bo-lo Champion (Junior Division) Award of Merit, three library cards, a parking ticket and his Barclaycard." That proof mostly demonstrates that the gentleman doth protest too much. As Shalinsky observes, "To think that you would go to so much trouble. What are you afraid of, Griffin?"

Mortimer's asserted identity indirectly but ironically relates to a secret neurotic fear. The title of the novel crudely emphasizes what the protagonist is not. Mortimer is certain that he is underendowed. His certainty is self-fulfilling, for his sense of sexual inadequacy soon translates into permanent impotence. Equally pertinent to the matter at hand, Mortimer also half believes prevailing superstitions about the impressive penile development of both Negroes and Jews. So an accusation of Jewishness should be a welcome charge. As we have already seen, it is not. Mortimer's rejection of Jewishness is, then, partly also an acceptance of impotence.

Even more self-demeaning and, ultimately, self-destructive, Mortimer's attempts to prove he is not Jewish, his anger at Shalinsky's interference in his life, and the charges of anti-Semitism that Mortimer's anger provokes from Shalinsky's more militant cohorts, all allow others to label Mortimer. "To his horror, he discovered he was now on the mailing list of more than one lunatic fringe group. The Sons of Poland, the Royal Hungarian Society, Fighters for a Free Ukraine, and other groups and unaffiliated persons long alert to the international Jewish conspiracy wrote with invitations to lecture and offers of help." And again Mortimer's denial of the charges only serves to confirm the accusation in the eyes of his "fellow" self-professed anti-Semites. A hint of anti-Semitism also serves to ingratiate him further with the Star Maker who, for obvious reasons, prefers to entrust his company's murderous business to the capable hands of ex-Nazis. And, as previously noted, the association with Star Maker ultimately proves to be the protagonist's undoing. When called upon to play a new role—callous, anti-Semitic, anti-humane —Mortimer again protests and wants to be, simply, Mortimer Griffin, Canadian, man of decent conscience. Mortimer did not profit from the honesty that kept him from accepting the role that Shalinsky repeatedly offered, and neither is he rewarded when he cannot be seduced into assuming the role that Star Maker would have him embrace. Quite the contrary —the Star Maker orders his assassination, an assassination that is imminent as the novel ends.

If all the world is a stage, then pity the man who cannot play a part. Mortimer's small attempts at self-dramatization all end comically, ineptly. We have Mortimer the non-Jew "Jew" and Mortimer the anti-anti-Semitic "anti-Semite." We might also note such matters as the impotent man's secret sexual treasure trove—a locked cabinet filled with aids for fornication and impediments to conception. In order to prove his manliness, Mortimer had begun to buy more and more sexual items from the apothecary shop owned by an old man who also drinks at the local pub that Mortimer frequents. Tales of the customer's purchases give him a certain credit in the bar. But he cannot manage even that sad pretense at potency. Furthermore, his masquerade as a secret swinger is a fantasy role that is forced on him as much by the limitations in the lives of the other patrons of the Eight Bells as by his own inadequacies. Indeed, the fantasy is soon taken out of his hands. If he does not regularly stop at the shop for the goods that he supposedly requires, the enterprising apothecary will bring them to the bar or even make an unannounced home delivery. Which leaves

Mortimer with a disposal problem, and he finds himself—old-fashioned again—carefully flushing things down toilets, furtively dropping pro- phylactics in the park, concealing "the evidence" deep in the garbage can. In short, his continuing impotence is mocked by his "evidence" to prove otherwise. The would-be "secret swinger" repeatedly demonstrates that he is very much a secret prude.

All of Mortimer's sexual misadventures in- volve playacting and hypocrisy, or, more accu- rately, his playacting and hypocrisy regularly turn on purported sexual misadventures. In order to cover his sentimental biweekly outings with Miss Ryerson, his old schoolteacher who has recently come to London, Mortimer pre- tends that he is having an affair with Rachel Coleman, the same beautiful black woman whom he first met so maladroitly at the bank. In order to convince his wife of his supposed infidelity he fills his pockets with old condom wrappers. He will contrive a kiss from his spin- sterly secretary and then have his wife find the lipstick-smudged handkerchief with which he wiped the kiss away. Such ruses work too well, especially when impotence becomes the final proof that he is having his fun elsewhere. Would-be-with-it Joyce, hitherto very much a prude herself, feels called upon to begin similar adventures on her own. Within twenty-four hours she falls into the grubby hands of Ziggy Spicehandler. Joyce, moreover, doing what Mortimer only played at doing, finds that she enjoys doing it. Soon she is omitting her morning bath, neglecting to shave her legs and armpits, even forsaking her can of bathroom deodorizer, and all the while cooing to Mortimer about how Ziggy has made her feel like a "real" and "natural" woman.

In contrast, Mortimer cannot consummate his affair with Rachel even when, physiologically speaking, he could. His impotence has temporarily abated; she is more than available; but he finds himself playing to her fantasies, not his own. First there is the matter of payment but not prostitution. He must give her a check for twenty-five pounds, not for services rendered, but "because this world being imperfect, this world being what it is, no ofay is capable of balling with a black girl without paying for it." She is "taking the bread" to assuage the guilt he would otherwise afterwards feel. Further demonstrating her principles, she soon has occasion to insist that she does not put out for "Jew boys," and "in the buff" there is a surefire test that will expose even those specimens attempting to pass. At which point, Mortimer, who had been circumsized, "whipped" his trousers on again and made a hasty retreat, the Jew in symbol if not in fact.

Considering his condition, Mortimer's final "partner," Polly Morgan, is also his ideal mate. Theirs is a match made in Hollywood. And in Polly's Hollywood existence, everything is show. Whether lovemaking or eating, artfully arranged images preclude any need for substance. So Mortimer finds himself sneaking sandwiches "in the toilet, for she was bound to cut from pon-

dering the sauce to serving coffee and brandy."
Sex, too, considering the movie censorship of the
early sixties, is a matter of before and after. Their
first time, he shuts his eyes in "anguish" when he
cannot quite bring himself to confess his impotence, and then opens them to find "her luxu-
riating on the bed, nude, sleepy-eyed, satiated."
"Was it super for you too, darling?" she naturally
asks:

> "Well, yes."
> "Was it never like this for you before?"
> *"No!"*
> "You're such a bad liar. I love you for that."
> "But I'm telling the truth, God damn it."
> "Yes, you are, that's exactly what I mean. If you
> were lying, I could tell from your face."

The conversation does not make sense, but then
neither does the setting. Mortimer still has his
clothes on; he knows that nothing has tran-
spired. Nonetheless, the tableau is as it should
be. The proper lines have been spoken.

The proper lines are all clichés: "Let's live
for love, Mortimer, you and I. . . . Let's not die for
it." Or, " 'When we are old,' she said, 'I want you
always to remember me like this, the sun catch-
ing fire in my hair. . . .' " Even love's setbacks are
according to script. After the make-believe
abortion that ends the make-believe pregnancy:
"As he had anticipated, she said, 'I feel dirty.' "
By then, however, Mortimer is entering into the
spirit of the game: "As was expected of him, he
replied, 'yes, I know,' but emptily." His only fear
is that, as movies were rapidly becoming in-

creasingly explicit, he might eventually be called upon to fill in the crucial gap between the dissolve "from his cupping a breast to the gratifying pillow talk that followed the most satisfying lovemaking." But meanwhile Mortimer happily settles for the world of appearances and the reality of illusory hopes. He and Polly are even "planning" to run off to Canada to start a new life.

Mortimer, an old hand at failed fantasy, readily follows Polly's lead, for she is much more adept in that business than he is. The master of fantasy in this novel is, however, the ominous Star Maker. As the name attests, this individual makes stars. Because stars made in the conventional sense proved too troublesome, they were made in a more mechanical and manageable manner. An assembled team of international scientists was ordered "to get into that lab and don't come out until you've made me a star." Movies, and particularly Mortimer's boyhood movie star idol, his image of what a man should be, were even more unreal than Mortimer imagined.

When Mortimer witnesses the desperate attempt of his old idol to escape the velvet-lined mothproofed box where that automaton— merely an expensive tool—is kept, deflated, until his next film, he sees that pretense has been pushed to the point of approximating truth. The automaton is almost human; it yearns for freedom, a wife, a normal life. As such, the Star is the converse of the Star Maker, who is also in his/her way a made man/woman. But not so well made; Star Maker's body, mismatched and grotesque, is a conglomerate of different spare parts that the spare-parts men and women could not always spare. It is the end product of abstract will and medical "art." And it will be pushed to a still further end when the union of Star Maker with Star Maker produces another Star Maker to be Star Maker's heir.

In a world where life can be prolonged unnaturally and produced so unnaturally, why should not extinction also sometimes be imposed prematurely and for profit? That question is the justification (except that Star Maker never needs a justification) for the timely deaths of the first two subjects—a has-been politician and a former actor—in Oriole Press's Our Living History biography series. Their lurid "suicides" (murders masquerading as self-slaughter) assure fantastic sales. The third book will do as well. "But he's so young," Dino protests when he is told whom the volume will portray and before he realizes the foolishness of his own sentimentality. After Dino's exit, when Mortimer will not take over Oriole Press and attend to business as required, he simply becomes the first subject of a new series, England Now. He, too, he realizes, will soon be history.

Cocksure is a devastating satire on England Now (circa 1965), on an imitation Hollywood world in which everyone is a con man. "Star Maker, Blessed Be His Name," is the god this shabby time deserves. He/she raises narcissism to hitherto undreamt of heights: " 'And it's fun, oh it's such fun. In all my years I have enjoyed nothing more than making love to me,' the Star Maker said, embracing, nuzzling upper arms, kissing, licking." Disgusting! Even pretty Polly is a siren on these shores, for her seemingly harmless games of fantasy prove fatal. Confronting an impending tragedy—Mortimer's death will preserve the secret of Star Maker's empire and enrich it at the same time—Polly can only indulge her own sense of drama. Sent to summon help, "Polly ran. She ran and ran. The first telephone booth she came to was empty, which wouldn't have done at all. She continued, breathless, to the next booth where, fortunately, a long-haired teen-ager was chattering endlessly, unaware that a man's life was at stake." Waiting is all. When she finally can place the call to the police, she does not do so. "On the wide screen that was her mind's eye" rescue has already arrived—just "in the nick of time," of course.

The satire can also be more subtle. We have already noted some ways in which Mortimer almost merits his putative identity. Other hints are also given in the novel, starting with such matters as his fancy for "chopped liver." But the essential and most significant reason is the simplest of all. Mortimer is chosen for the role. He is chosen by Shalinsky, who answers the other's final assertion that he is not Jewish with, "But Griffin, Griffin, don't you see? A Jew is an idea. Today you're my idea of a Jew." The logic is impeccable, even though Mortimer would refuse the honor offered. He might have done better to have accepted it, since, through another of Richler's effective ironies, a Jew and the only self-confessed con man in the novel is also the only morally admirable character. Shalinsky calculatingly plays whatever role is required, sitting in waiting rooms of rich co-religionists, for example, hawking, sucking his teeth, "trading" on the fact that he is an "embarrassment," to elicit some contribution whereby he can both keep his magazine *Jewish Thought* afloat and also send some aid, canned food and writing supplies, to the Jewish poets behind the Iron Curtain. As Shalinsky explains to Mortimer, in the course of their final conversation, explaining, in the process, the impending threat to Mortimer's life, "Well, now you see, now you know. It's hard to be a Jew." Mortimer still does not really know, but, chosen by both Shalinsky and the Star Maker, he soon will.

It must, however, be acknowledged that in some respects *Cocksure* is a flawed novel. The different strands of the plot and the various satiric targets are not all of a piece. The excesses of sixties' childrearing—reading, for example, bedtime stories from an illustrated *Hiroshima* to teach little Dougie what toy guns lead to—is too easy a target and, moreover, is hardly consistent with the different order of public make-believe whereby most of the characters conduct their lives. Neither can we take very seriously, or very comically, the Beatrice Webb School with its Christmas play of *Philosophy in the Bedroom,* as performed by nude and gawky ten-year-olds. The humor is sometimes sophomoric and centered on an adolescent concern with sex as conceived by adolescents.[2] Witness the modus operandi (Friday afternoon sexual favors for the four top students) whereby Miss Ryerson, Mortimer's old and old-fashoined teacher, hired at Beatrice Webb House, finally manages to encourage decorum and study at that bastion of progressive miseducation. We can note her comparative success in the brave new world of Old England, as compared to her former student's failures, yet the whole episode is definitely a lower order of comedy than that which characterizes Mortimer's own amorous misadventures.

Seeing these inconsistencies on even the largest level of the plotting of the novel, George Woodcock argues:

It is not that the Star Maker and Shalinsky are intrinsically implausible companions, or that the action is unconvincing in satiric terms. It is rather that there is no real fusion of tone between the sticky confusion of Mortimer's private life and the sinister silliness he encounters in the company of the Star Maker. It is as if a character were living in two novels.[3]

And yet one could reply that of course Mortimer lives in two novels, in two worlds. We have the "real life" trials of Mortimer Griffin as husband, father, and non-Jewish Jew; we have the satirical exaggerations of Star Maker and his entourage, including Polly ever at the movies. There is, admittedly, a disjunction between these worlds but, as I have already shown, there is not really such a difference between them. On the contrary, the main point of Richler's Swiftian satire is to intimate that the grotesque surrealistic world of the Star Maker or of the Beatrice Webb School is but the *reductio ad absurdum* of the "real" world of mod London in the sixties, which, on the private and public level, has its own "sinister silliness" too.

8

St. Urbain's Horseman: The Protagonist on Trial

St. Urbain's Horseman *is longer,* denser, and more complexly plotted than any of the novels that preceded it. It is Richler's magnum opus. Yet the work that is obviously intended to be the culmination of Richler's art as a novelist up to that point is just as obviously tied to the fiction that came before. Like *The Acrobats* and *A Choice of Enemies, St. Urbain's Horseman* is a story of an artist—somewhat *manqué*—searching, in uneasy exile, for his own identity. Like *Son of a Smaller Hero, St. Urbain's Horseman* is a modified Canadian-Jewish *bildungsroman,* a story of how the protagonist is shaped by his time, his place, and—a central theme in all of Richler's more serious fiction—his family. Furthermore, the two families in the two novels just named are much the same: a weak father, a manipulating mother, uncles who carry the weight that the father lacks. Then, too, in *St. Urbain's Horseman,* as in *The Incomparable Atuk* and *Cocksure,* the grotesqueries of modern manners and contemporary culture are satirically exaggerated. Yet it must be admitted that the satiric elements in the later novel are occasional and naturalistic, not essential and surrealistic, which is to say that the book is more in the vein of *The Apprenticeship of Duddy Kravitz*, a basically realistic work, with moral (individual) and social (group) portraits highlighted by deft satiric touches.

The comparison to *Duddy Kravitz* is particularly germane. The prospective endeavor of the young man on the make in the earlier work is balanced by the retrospective assessment of how the definitely arrived middle-aged protagonist of *St. Urbain's Horseman* made it. In each case we have the trials that beset the central character (and the trials that he makes for those around him), the pitfalls into which he appropriately falls, and his ironically limited final success. Even more to the point, in each novel there is an ironically limited protagonist with discordant qualities—positive and negative—that, although relatively easy to identify, are hard to add up. Furthermore, the two novels are connected through characters who appear in both. We first meet Jacob Hersh, the protagonist of *St. Urbain's Horseman*, in Room 41 of Fletcher's Field High School at the beginning of *The Apprenticeship of Duddy Kravitz*. But not until the end of the novel does he play even a minor role in the book. Jake is one of the few old Fletcher's Field schoolfellows who remains friends with Duddy. Then, early in *St. Urbain's Horseman*, we encounter the final chapters of how Duddy made his rise, if not to fame, at least to fortune. At the end of the novel we also see him, a millionaire now, amply repay Jacob Hersh for the friendship that Jake had earlier shown him—at the end of *The Ap-*

prenticeship of Duddy Kravitz and the beginning of *St. Urbain's Horseman.* In effect, each character serves as a kind of ironic parenthesis enclosing the story of the other.

There is still another way in which the earlier fiction, taken together, anticipates *St. Urbain's Horseman.* As I have already noted, all of Richler's novels have a moral focus. Even the absurdist comedy of *The Incomparable Atuk* and *Cocksure* is firmly grounded in a clear awareness of what is wrong with the world and with most of the characters portrayed in those two works. The moral focus, of course, can be considerably more complex than simply an exaggerating mirror held up to the foibles of the time. In Richler's best realistic fiction there is a kind of multifocal effect, a blurring of image that emphasizes the problems of judging. We are required to come to some estimation of Noah or Norman or Duddy, and we are also shown how hard it is to do so fairly. In short, Richler judges the reader's propensity to judge precipitously, to resort to ready, simplistic categories in order to classify complicated human behavior. Certainly Noah should do what every literary portrait of the artist as a young man prescribes and bravely strike out to fulfill his own anticipated destiny. Yet, by so doing, he probably kills his mother. Obviously Duddy is a *pusherke.* And just as obviously, he is more than just a *pusherke,* and, because he is more, he is somehow even less when he can only see—and use—in best *pusherke* fashion, those, like Yvette, who can see—and love—the man behind the mask. But difficult as Duddy's case is,

Jake's is still more so. Nevertheless, as even a cursory reading of the novel demonstrates, Jake must be judged. The problem, as previously noted, is to do so justly, and that, in a nutshell, is Jake's problem too.

The implicit concern with moral judgments that informs the earlier fiction is made explicit in *St. Urbain's Horseman*. Indeed, Richler most appropriately structures the novel around a trial—a trial on a morals charge. The book begins with the trial underway. It ends with a verdict rendered, several verdicts in fact. But the legal proceeding, as Zailig Pollock notes, "is more than just the climax [and core] of the novel; it provides a central metaphor around which all the issues of the novel are organized."[1] Jake is on trial, and that trial tries his wife, his friends, and the family that he thought he left behind in Canada (especially his mother). The trial tries him in another sense too, for it is clearly the objective correlative to and direct consequence of his own middle-age identity crisis. His professional status is also called into question, a question that is even more pointed in that he is both unemployed and well-paid during the time of the trial. A director of TV scripts and a would-be movie director, he has achieved, shortly before the novel begins, his greatest success, which was to be fired from the movie that he was hired to direct but to go on receiving the salary that his contract promised. But most of all, Jake must be both the prosecutor and defendant in his own private judicial process as, a Jewish expatriate Canadian, quite out of place in court at Old

Bailey, he reviews the past that brought him to that pass.

The rather simple structure of the novel expresses this process of review. Scenes from the present are juxtaposed with scenes from the past. That juxtaposition, it should be noted, is not the thematically significant interplay of past and present that almost imagistically conveys the meaning of a work such as Joseph Conrad's *Lord Jim.* As John Moss observes of *St. Urbain's Horseman:* "Chronology is a convenience for Richler, rather than a major plot device. Flashbacks and forward flow simply allow the author to work in the necessary details."[2] Yet the novel is neither so straightforward nor so simple as this quotation suggests. Those "necessary details" are also often loaded details whereby Jake envisions one version of his story while the reader can envision quite a different version.

The story, in its basic outlines, is quite clear. Jake, born into one of the poorer branches of a successful Jewish family (but one still restricted to the St. Urbain Street Montreal ghetto), yearns for a larger, freer life. Canada is, for him and in W.H. Auden's words, *tiefste Provinz,* "the remotest hinterland." The source of the label suggests Jake's aspirations. He wants, as a socially engaged artist, to make his mark in the larger world. The field for that endeavor will be, he first imagines, New York City. But at the border he is confused with a cousin, Joey Hersh, whom Jake already very much admires. Jake's evaluation of Joey is not shared by the American officials. Deemed an undesirable immigrant and denied entry in the United States—a mistake that his ready mouth does not help to resolve—Jake must opt for England. With a like-minded friend, Luke Scott, a young Canadian would-be writer from an impeccable WASP background, Jake soon leaves Montreal for London.

Success, Luke's success, subsequently mars the friendship. The career of the one soars while the career of the other merely rolls along to, finally, a thousand pounds a week for not working, an ambiguous success that most men well might envy, but one that certainly does not satisfy Jake. Still, he does score one early triumph over Luke. When they both compete for the same girl, she chooses Jake. He is most lucky in her choice. Nancy is beautiful, sensitive, intelligent, sane. She is one of Richler's few believable women, which is all the more surprising since she is a close-to-perfect wife.[3] Nevertheless, Jake is not satisfied. Even though, on one level, he knows he could not be happier, he still cannot fully accept his personal happiness, anymore than he can be content with his more obviously limited professional success. He fantasizes Nancy's infidelities, foresees his three children turning against him, imagines his own immediate and grotesque demise from cancer of the rectum. He also takes up with a most dubious character, an obvious psychopath who comes into Jake's life to extort a substantial sum of money and remains to be a "friend." Playing with fire, Jake is burned. It is this friend, Harry Stein, who engineers the sexual misadventure that leads to the trial underway when the book begins. Not until the final chapters do we discover what that misadventure was, how it came to the law's attention, what the charges were, and how the jury finds.

The relationships between Jake, on the one hand, and Joey Hersh and Harry Stein, on the other, present the careful reader with one of the most difficult problems of interpretation in the novel. The problem is, to start with, why do these two play such a large role in Jake's life? One is surprised that Harry, after he is paid off, plays any role at all. And Joey, glamorized during Jake's rebellious adolescence, continues to be for Jake almost a mythic hero long after all the available evidence should have suggested quite another judgment. On the trail of his cousin's supposed heroic exploits—he imagines Joey as the Horseman, an avenger of the Jews determined to track down and kill Dr. Mengele, the Nazi officer reponsible for selecting those who were to be sent to the gas chambers at Auschwitz—Jake continually runs up against evidence of quite different activities. Joey abandoned a wife and child in Israel; he smuggled hashish to NATO troops in Germany; in England he conned, through the promise of marriage, a gullible and not very bright middle-aged Jewish widow, Ruthy Flam, out of her life's savings. And, because of Ruthy, Jake, on Joey's trail, soon finds Harry on his. A man bitterly resentful of his low station in life, Harry viciously strikes out at all those who represent unfairness, unfairness to Harry. He cloaks his rancor in the rhetoric of social justice, but as one critic rightly points out,

"Harry's vaunted egalitarianism can function in just one fashion: he is willing to stamp on Jew [Harry, too, is Jewish] and gentile alike. He is the stuff of which the Sonderkommando were made."[4] Harry, appointing himself Ruthy's protector, decides that the "loan" made by Ruthy to Joey shoud be repaid by Jake. He, for all practical purposes, extorts the repayment. Then, when Jake still offers friendship, Harry repays him by involving Jake in an unusual *ménage à trois* with Ingrid Loebner, a German *au pair* girl, from which Jake emerges charged with sodomy, with aiding and abetting an indecent assault, and with possession of marijuana. The logic of this whole progress is retrospectively obvious to its perpetrator and victim:

> Jake was not surprised that out of his obsession with the Horseman he had been delivered Ruthy.
> Who had sent him Harry.
> Who had served him Ingrid.

The plotting of the novel, Harry as a consequence of Joey, emphasizes the connection between the two. But the two characters are conjoined by more than the plot. There is a thematic connection also, for both Joey and Harry are equally expressions of a basic element, a basic flaw even, in Jake's character. That flaw is clear in his past, which was dominated by Joey, and in his present, when he is taken in by Harry. Briefly put, Jake prefers the comfort and the crutch of a substitute self. He sees in another the image of what he desires, or fears, and then solves his own problems of being by contemplating what his projected double did, does, or might do. This process is particularly obvious with Joey, who rides into Jake's life when the latter is enduring a restrained and static adolescent rebellion. To the teenager yearning for the larger world, the older cousin—a former minor league baseball player, a boxer, a one-time movie actor, a pilot—is all that the younger one would be. And Joey then becomes even more of a model when he takes an active role in resisting the local French-Canadian anti-Semitism of the time. "What are you going to do about it?" he asks the other residents of St. Urbain Street, when Jewish children are bullied on the school playground or when an older youth is beaten up at a French dance hall. Led by Joey, they do something. Understandably, Jake idolizes his cousin. Yet his idolizing also has its darker side. Because he cannot fully believe in his own prospective revolt, he insists on believing in Joey's. Thus the determination with which he clings, despite much contrary evidence, to his vision of Joey—the Horseman who will "do something" about the wrongs of the world on the largest level. Joey is the man that Jake would be, and, as long as Joey is that man, Jake does not have to become the Horseman himself. Indeed, he does not have to admit the fact that, really, he cannot even ride.

The same process, in reverse, is played out later with Harry. Jake, as an adolescent, could not fully believe in his own envisioned future. When, as a middle-aged man, he has achieved considerable success (but success, as previously noted, that is pointedly ambiguous), he cannot completely believe in that success either. His rise to considerable wealth and fame elicits a continuing preoccupation with his still enduring failures. Thus, "I will be buried without ever having directed Olivier," he at one time muses, without ever having "made a film of the Benye Krick stories" or "cast Lauren Bacall in a thriller." These envisioned artistic limitations are mixed with other setbacks more mundane. Jake also laments that he will not have "had a black girl" or a "homosexual experience" or "met Mao" or "killed a Nazi." He will not have been "a prime minister," and neither will he have "rejected a knighthood" nor "delivered my speech turning down the Academy Award." Those last items are the most symptomatic of them all. It is not the honor but the grander stand of turning it down that would, he imagines, distinguish him. So the whole catalogue represents, as one critic rightly observes, "experience transformed into the self-serving commodities of a competitive and acquisitive society."[5] And since "value derives from . . . rarity, from the envy felt by those denied these experiences," it follows that experience envisioned promises fulfillment but vision experienced loses its value.[6] In short, and this is a quality of both Jake and his world, the obverse of the earlier dream of success is the subsequent dream of failure. Man's reach must exceed his grasp or what is dreaming for? Making it is, by definition, not making it enough, which prompts a new version of the earlier dream: "Even failure or disaster may be cher-

ished or envied if only it is spectacular or grotesque enough."[7] Yet Jake cannot wholly dedi-
cate himself to that end either. Total failure is a
serious business, so he temporizes and projects.
Just as Joey earlier was his substitute success,
now Harry can allow for a vicarious failure. Jake
cast Harry (Jake is, remember, a director) in the
role he wants him to play, a decent down-and-
outer understandably embittered by the dis-
apointments he must bear. Significantly, the
friendly diminutive by which he addresses
Harry, "Hershel," means, of course, "little
Hersh."[8] Joey is Jake in the grand heroic mold,
while Harry is the much smaller model, and the
one that does not work.

Harry, as failure, serves still another function. He ties Jake to his past and particularly to
its more humbling and galling aspects. It is not at
all surprising that the first consequence of Jake's
arrest is the arrival of Mrs. Hersh in London to
"help out" by imposing herself and her fear of
impending death (Jake's father has just died) on
her son and his wife. Yet the hints of age and
death brought in by Mrs. Hersh are balanced, it
should be noted, by the fact of birth. Nancy has
just borne to Jake their third child. Such details
themselves, the death of his father, the presence
of his elderly mother who regularly expostulates
on the burdens of parenthood, the birth of his
second son, fix Jake thoroughly in midlife and
remind him that he is a product of the background that he has not escaped. "What am I
doing here?" he asks of London and not just of
the Old Bailey courtrooms. That question is

given even more point by the fact that immediately before the crucial events of the novel
Jake returned to Canada to sit shiva (the Jewish
mourning ceremony) after the death of his
father. Back in the city of his birth, he found
himself sentimentally attracted to the world of
Montreal Jews because, unlike trendy England,
in this world there were values that still worked.

He sees how comfortable and human the
traditional close-knit family life—now liberated
from the ghetto—really is. He sees again some of
the same old limitations that originally inspired
his determination to flee St. Urbain Street. In
brief, he is deeply ambivalent about the partly
changed old life to which he no longer belongs.
He is also aware of how his Montreal relatives
must view him. The success who embodies all
that he despises in mod London, he is their "Fab
Goy." The position pinches. Jake, who enjoys
being a satirical commentator on the foibles of
others, does not like it when the tables are turned
and he is the object of evaluation—especially
when he is judged by those who lead the life he
worked so hard to escape. In anger he accuses
one uncle, the most successful member of the
Canadian branch of the family, of ending Joey's
Montreal sojourn by betraying the nephew to
the police. He subsequently physically attacks
the fat, crude young cousin who stands to inherit
this uncle's fortune. Then, doubting himself and
almost disgusted by what he has just done, he
leaves.Montreal a day early. Arriving home un-
expectedly, he finds Harry and Ingrid in the

midst of their little sexual circus, and soon thereafter finds himself arrested and in court.

As the novel opens, Jake is busy fleeing the self-indulgent attentions of his mother as well as the accusing yet sympathetic eyes of his wife, who tries to retain some personal dignity in the face of her husband's impending court case and the attendant scandal. It is not until the final portions of the novel that we learn the exact nature of the scandal and what the charges were. With these revelations we can also understand the various puzzling references that Richler has dropped, seemingly gratuitously, throughout the novel—the saddle, the riding crop, the satirically pornographic script. All this material evidence in the court case is ultimately explained, and what seems in the courtroom to demonstrate Jake's depravity really proves no such thing. But to return to the crime, the bare facts of the case are as follows: Jake Hersh returns from his father's funeral, depressed and anxious, continually rehashing the events of the preceding week and trying to prove to himself that he has not been quite the fool he knows he has been. While away, and contrary to a promise he made to Nancy, who is with the children at their summer cottage, he has allowed Harry to stay in the house, presumably to use it as a prop for seduction, since Harry's own dank and dirty basement quarters will hardly serve the same purpose. Harry, however, has appropriated not only Jake's residence but his professional identity as well. Passing himself off as Jake Hersh, film director, he has picked up a pretty girl at a local coffeehouse and invited her back for a screen test. The script is a mildly pornographic satire on the English that Luke and Jake once wrote. One episode in "The Good Britons" requires General Montgomery to be encouraged to fight the Germans by a little flagellation administered by an undressed Mary Poppins. So Jake walks in on what could well be called a casting party. The method reading that Harry, as pseudo-director, required has led, as Harry hoped, to some method acting.

When Jake returns, he encounters, first, the naked girl, Ingrid. He tells her who he is and that he owns the house and then retires to his room. He is undressing to go to bed (alone) when Ingrid enters, still naked and carrying a tray of brandy. She briefly tries to seduce him. He considers the possibility but only momentarily and orders her from his room. Several hours later he is awakened by the sound of laughter and goes down to find Harry and Ingrid still at play. Once more Ingrid tries to seduce him; once more he momentarily acquiesces, but only momentarily. Then, angry, he pushes her from him and begins to condemn her and her family as Germans. Informed that he is Jewish, she responds that she "would not have guessed," he was being "so nice." Now furious at that unconscious racial slur (Jews can normally be recognized by how "unnice" they are), Jake preemptively orders the woman from the house, bruising her arm and her ego in the process. Harry demurs; Jake insists; Ingrid hastily dresses and flees, weeping, out into the early morning street to be picked up by two patrolling police officers to whom she tells an almost incoherent tale of having been drugged, raped, and sodomized. She has been smoking marijuana; she had also been told that she would lose her job the next time she stayed out all night. She needs a story, and so she embellishes rather freely on what had happened. But when she tries to end the matter with the story and go home, the police insist that laws have been broken, that arrests must be made. Rather than admit her exaggerations, Ingrid acquiesces to the prosecution of the two men. After all, Harry deceived her, and Jake humiliated her. Let the bastards pay.

There is something a little coy about this whole situation. Richler seems to be too intent on proclaiming that his protagonist, although a moral man, is definitely no prude. Perhaps, however, we are to see the whole misadventure as demonstrating another contradiction in Jake's own makeup. He definitely does not cut a very impressive figure when he is required to testify in court that it felt "soothing" to have Miss Loebner "stroke [his] penis." But there is still the larger contradiction between the serious moral tone of the whole work and the sex and scandal-sheet trial around which it is organized. By deploying throughout the novel various (and generally juicy) details of the orgy that led to the trial, Richler manages to have his "cheesecake" and deplore it too. At the same time, however, the trial fits perfectly into the plot. It is Jake's obsession with Joey that brings him back early to London and to Harry (another legacy from

Joey), who serves him Ingrid, whom—a sad representative of the German problem—he must reject. All the issues of his past and present are brought into focus. The trial also effectively serves to explore the character of its various participants. Richler's careful handling of narrative perspective allows us to judge each witness's account of what happened against a relatively objective description of what did, in fact, occur. Finally, the trial graphically demonstrates the real charge against Jake. He is in court not for anything that he actually did to Ingrid, but because of his relationship with Harry.

At this point it might be helpful to look more closely at Jake's involvement with Harry. I would begin by insisting that Jake is not attracted to Harry because of the latter's (in one critic's phrase) "irrepressibly disreputable" nature.[9] "Irrepressibly disreputable" better describes a Falstaff than a Harry Stein. Richler goes to considerable detail to emphasize how unappealing Harry is. We have a number of otherwise gratuitous details, such as an account of how Harry surreptitiously scratched a parked and unattended Rolls Royce all along one side and then, seeing that he was still unobserved, returned to deface the other side too. He several times promoted bomb scares and once tried to kill (by disconnecting the brakes on her car) an actress who, solicited on the telephone, spurned his attentions. This is no genial joker, appealing because of his quaintly low ways. Jake, moreover, knows as much. When Harry first comes calling, to collect Ruthy's debt, that whole exercise loudly proclaims itself as extortion. When Harry leaves after the first visit, Jake notes the cigarette hole that his visitor burnt in a new and expensive chair. But what is still more notable is Jake's reaction: "Why, the bastard, Jake thought, with sneaking admiration, he did it on purpose."

Jake grudgingly admires Harry even when he is the target of Harry's insults and assaults. He identifies with Harry, as already noted, and sees the other as an exaggerated image of himself as a defiant failure. That identification is partly encouraged by the obvious similarities of the two: "they are of the same age, they come from similar harsh urban backgrounds, and they share the same Jewish-centered awareness of the world's cruelty."[10] They share something more too. As Harry insists to Jake, "The problem is I'm not getting enough—I'm not getting enough of *anything*." Jake feels the same way. So Harry mirrors Jake's gripes against the world, gripes that the latter must maintain rather surreptitiously, since he has obviously done very well in the world he chooses to scorn. He has a beautiful wife, three children, an elegant house in the suburbs, all the supposed prerequisites for a good life. Jake is even paid more in one month for *not* working than Harry is paid in a year for working as an accountant, an accountant who, ironically, is employed by the firm that does Jake's taxes. And one of Harry's ploys, as he tries to persuade Jake to come up with Ruthy's money, is to report Jake's tax dodges to the revenue officials. Trials are brewing for Jake on several different fronts.

The resolution of the novel abounds with characteristic Richler ironies. To start with, Harry, who intended to get Jake into legal trouble, does not at all intend the legal trouble into which he gets him. Their previous roles are substantially reversed when Harry wishes to placate Jake on his unexpected return to London and prompts Ingrid to invite the reluctant host of their little party to join the fun. When Jake, furious at both of them, orders Ingrid out of the house, it is Harry who sounds, incongruously, the voice of reason and wants to calm the insulted girl. Such inconsistencies continue throughout the court proceedings. Harry, at the trial, insists that it is class that will decide the issue, and then, called to testify, he belligerently plays the defiant hooligan. He goes so far to impress the jury with his low class status that he even manages to bring up himself his past criminal record, which would otherwise have been inadmissible evidence. He finally softens toward Jake after Jake pays for his legal defense and, on the witness stand, lies for him. "You've been a friend to me, just like you said," he admits. Then, when his predictions about class prove true (Jake gets fined and Harry gets seven years), he attempts, with a sudden flurry of his own lies, to send Jake to prison with him. The vendetta continues from prison. Harry tries to destroy Jake's marriage, writing Nancy grotesquely detailed letters about what the three of them—he, Jake, and Ingrid—"really" did and how a different threesome—Jake, Nancy, and Harry—will carry on once he gets out. Perhaps the largest irony in the trial is the manner in which, on the basis of perjured testimony, Harry receives the harsh sentence that he thoroughly deserves.

Harry merits the sentence he receives, but not just for the reasons that prompt the jury to convict him. In his own eyes, of course, he is innocent. And therein lies his real guilt and the reason why the author emphasizes his repeated deceptions and self-deceptions, his tendency to justify his own violations against humanity with the self-pitying pretense that he was only "getting even." Furthermore, if Ingrid is foolish, selfish, and gullible enough to indulge in sex for possible fame and profit, then, so far as Harry is concerned, she surely deserves the misfortunes she is prey to. The results of his actions—disconnecting brakes, making bomb threats, or abusing young women—are never *his* fault, but are really the fault of a society that puts him into the position of having to deceive. But, since he really puts himself into all his offensive positions, he is, as the judge accurately notes, "a humbug ... and a troublemaker of the most reprehensible sort." Besides, the sodomy did take place, so Harry is technically guilty of one of the two charges for which he is sentenced, and, with his past record, one charge would serve as well as two to put him away.

Thematically, the self-pitying Harry with the grudge against the world is connected to that side of Jake whereby he, too, views himself—

despite all evidence to the contrary—as the perpetual victim (of Germans, of uppercrust British,
of crass commercial tastes, of the older generation, of the younger generation). This distorted
self-view also prompts him to hire perpetual
misfits for his few productions, as if occasionally
hanging out with society's rejects makes him
exempt from their scorn—innocence by association. Furthermore, Jake, as victim, as Jew, need
not feel guilt or responsibility for the world
around him. Quite the contrary, his fantasies
—shades of Joey *and* Harry—are fantasies of
revenge, reactive but not revolutionary. For one
of his social position and profession, the fantasies are as self-indulgent as they are ineffectual.
So the final interaction with Ingrid deftly serves
to reveal the paltriness of Jake's aspirations to
retributive justice.

Early in the novel Richler describes a pho-
tograph that, for Jake, epitomizes the appalling
inhumanity of the Nazis. It is a picture of a
"beautiful Jewess" victim of the Germans, who,
stripped and crouched before a burial pit, was
"staring right into the camera without anger or
reproach . . . attempting to conceal her pen-
dulous breasts with her hands." Ingrid, when
Jake first sees her, strikes a similar pose.[11] The
connection becomes more overt when the young
woman, on coming into Jake's room, mentions
the gun she has seen. He tells her he has it to
"shoot some Germans. Maybe you." And then he
does more than threaten. After stripping her of
the shawl she is wearing, "just to show he wasn't
utterly unappreciative or a prude, he ran his

hand over her breasts and passed it angrily between her legs. Glaring at him, she locked him there. Jake, to his astonishment, responded by pinching her as viciously as he could." The resultant bruise becomes evidence that later partly proves an assault. If Jake's action here is not quite the kind of assault that the jury had in mind when they found him guilty, it is not exactly a love pinch either. But, more to the point, there has been a strange transmogrification in his moral universe. The beautiful Jewess gives way to the callow young German girl. The vision of the avenging Horseman rightly punishing Dr. Mengele is reduced to this ludicrous scene in which a rather sexually aroused Jewish man, without conscious intent, inflicts a most ambiguous pinch on the private parts of a nude Miss Loebner, who has herself already been thoroughly conned and used.

I earlier noted a crucial progression: Joey, through Ruthy, brought Harry, who then "served" Jake Ingrid. That progression can be extended one step further to complete one of the circles traced out in the novel. Harry, through Ingrid, brings back Joey again. Jake's treatment of Ingrid is all premised on the fact that she is German. Even though she was, as she tells him when he asks, born too late to have been in even the *Hitler Jugend*, he still makes her the embodiment of German guilt. Which allows him to play, at last, in a distinctly minor key, the envisioned role of Joey; he will be the Horseman dealing out vengeance for the suffering of his people. No matter that the object of that vengeance is a girl too young to have participated in the crime and with problems enough already. No matter that the Joey Jake plays is not Joey the Horseman but Joey the gigolo, Joey the abuser of various women. All that saves Jake from being more of a moral failure is the fact that his vengeance—a hard pinch, pitching the girl out —is as petty and insignificant as the occasion that allowed it.[12] Again the court's judgment is more valid than it might at first appear. As the judge makes clear, Jake is found guilty not so much for what he has technically done, but for the way he has done it. "You have been a confounded fool, Hersh." The magistrate goes on to observe that only "folly, and sheer egoism, perhaps" could explain Jake's "association" with Stein—or, it might be added, his treatment of Ingrid.

St. Urbain's Horseman is a complex novel. For the most part it is very well done. The ironies, the ambiguities, the tensions between Jake and his two different doppelgängers are all tightly controlled.[13] But the novel does have a few weaknesses and, especially at the end, some dubious sleight of hand is obvious. Richler, for example, can appropriately and conveniently dispose of Harry, thanks to the injust justice of the judge. The corresponding disposal of Joey, however, rings false. Convenience and coincidence are both strained when, immediately after the trial, Jake reads the letter informing him that his cousin has died in South America. Joey drops from the action through a demand for symmetry and a fortuitous air crash, not through the logic of events in the plot. Consider also the gun that Jake, at the very end of the novel, finds in Joey's old saddle (a souvenir that he had picked up from Ruthy), Jake's gesture toward suicide, and then the shot at the wall that leaves no mark. The weapon was "an actor's gun" that "only fires blanks." It is a gun too loaded with symbolic significance. Too loaded too is the long Biblical quotation beginning:

I am the Lord thy God, which brought thee out of the land of Egypt, from the house of bondage.
Thou shalt have none other gods before me.
Thou shalt not make thee any graven image.

Jake, as an Aaron-figure, has obviously worshipped some false idols, and we do not need the Bible to tell us so. Or does the quotation hint as to the future; is the erstwhile maker of graven images "to become the priest of the Most High, the first rabbi," the true artist?[14] If so, little in the novel supports that fond prediction. Certainly Jake's final epiphany, given immediately before the Biblical passage, "What if the Horseman was a distorting mirror and we each took the self-justifying image we required of him?" bespeaks no new depth of vision or breadth of understanding.

The promise of the future is, for Jake, on quite a lower level. Luke and Jake are reconciled; Jake will direct Luke's next script; that night, "for the first time since the trial's end, Jake and Nancy make love, shy with each other." Realizing, however, that the ending was verging on the saccharine, Richler altered the tenor of the last few paragraphs of the final chapter. The novel opened with Jake's dream of the Horseman, Joey "come" to "take" Dr. Mengele. It ends with Jake's "nightmare," in which "he was the Horseman now," fulfilling, in his dream, the dream he had earlier dreamt for Joey. He wakes from that dream to go to his attic study, in which he has kept all the accoutrements of his secret fantasy life, to take out the "horseman's journal" and change his last entry. "Died July 20, 1967, in an air crash" is crossed out; "presumed dead" is written in. Then Jake can return to sleep and to Nancy, partially protected, in best Jake fashion, from the responsibilities of his dream. Joey just might still be alive, which means that Jake still does not have to give up his vicariously self-indulgent vision of the Horseman or shoulder himself the demanding role that he has cast for Joey. The dream turned into nightmare can be turned back to harmless dream, despite the harm that that dream has done to Jake and his family.

We end, then, very much where we began. Richler gives us a portrait of a midcentury man caught in various middles. None of the dichotomies confronting Jake has been resolved. Probably none can be resolved. Canada, for Jake, is still the provinces, while England ever remains foreign territory. Jake has viewed his whole "generation" as "being squeezed between two raging and carnivorous ones, the old and resentful have-everythings and the young know-nothings ... it followed inevitably that, once having stumbled, he would be judged by one when accused by the other. Ingrid would sing, Mr. Justice Beal would pronounce." The young girl has sung; the older judge has pronounced; Jake and his other middle-aged associates are still "always the wrong age. Ever observers, never participants. The whirlwind elsewhere." Jake is also still caught between a desire for success and the allure of failure. He will direct Luke's play, but he cannot believe in it. They are all, Luke, Jake, and Nancy, only "ostensibly ... overjoyed" with the venture. In fact, Jake can direct the play only because he does not have to. Duddy has just advanced him ten thousand dollars, and so he no longer needs the opportunity that Luke offers, for, if he needed it, his pride would never allow him to accept it. He is still self-divided, and so is his immediate family. His heritage, he knows, is not his children's heritage. When, for example, he tries to convince himself that their rigorously unreligious Christmas tree is merely a pagan festivity symbol, he has to admit that, if he covered it with chicken fat, it would still be a Christmas tree, and yet the children have their tree. The contradictions remain. The ambiguities abound. In the last analysis, they serve to give us a convincing portrait of an essentially decent man hopelessly entangled in the problems of being human, one of which is the very human propensity to make problems for oneself.

9

Joshua Then and Now,
or The Trial Revisited

George Woodcock, in a 1971 discursive review of
St. Urbain's Horseman and the accomplishment
of the author up to that point, argued that
Richler had finally conjoined his two previously
disparate artistic sides—the "fantastic-satirist"
who mocked the inanities of modern popular
culture (and particularly the movies), as opposed to the "rather realistic urban novelist"
whose subject matter was the Jewish ghetto of
his boyhood Montreal. That "synthesis," Woodcock further suggested, "seems to mark the end
of a particular cycle in his [Richler's] work."[1]
"The wheel of exile" turned full circle promised,
according to this critic, either subsequent "self-
parody" or a "new [fictional] beginning."[2] But
the wheel of exile has since been given a few
additional turns, and *Joshua Then and Now,*
Richler's most recent novel and a work not published until nine years after the preceding *St.
Urbain's Horseman,* is neither a clear new
beginning nor an obvious self-parody. Instead, a
new twist—a comic resolution—is provided to a
standard Richler plot, spun out by the whirligig
of time and the exigencies of uncertain exile.

The connections between the two novels just mentioned are numerous. Both books, for example, are prefaced with epigraphs from W. H. Auden. Both partly turn on sexually loaded indiscretions that are progressively revealed and, more important, progressively redefined, so that each protagonist is finally not so much publicly guilty of his ostensible transgression as privately guilty of a sin rather different from the one for which he originally stood charged. The similarities between the two protagonists and their not coincidental resemblance to their creator, are also obvious:

Jake Hersh and Joshua Shapiro are both coeval with their creator. They are given quasi-creative occupations—Jake is a film director; Joshua a sports columnist, a television personality, and the author of several books. Both drink a lot, have lovely gentile wives and happy family lives. Both are tough, sardonic, and drolly neurotic on the outside, good-hearted and humane within. In the present time of their novels, both have reached a crisis point in middle age, the precipitates of which are gradually disclosed.[3]

But Kerry McSweeney is not so accurate when he goes on to postulate the equivalent "high seriousness of both characters' *crise*" or to balance Jake's "*idee fixe* about Germans and Jews," as indicated by his "obsession with Dr. Mengele in the jungles of Paraguay," with "Joshua's obsessive memory of Dr. Dr. Mueller, the ex-Nazi whom he had encountered during a stay on Ibiza in the early 1950s."[4] The actual Dr.

Mengele can more than sustain the significance that Jake imputes to him. Indeed, part of Jake's problem is the tragic fact that Mengele embodies an evil beyond measure and thus beyond the possibility of any calculated retributive justice. There was, of course, no real Dr. Dr. Mueller, and, more to the point, the fictional character is no embodiment of Nazi evil either. The reduplicated honorific Dr. Dr. ("I have two doctorates. Both awarded in Vienna. It is the custom there to use both titles") is only one of the numerous hints that Joshua's old nemesis was mostly pose and fraud. What is played up in one novel is played down in the other, and that is true of the two crises as well. As I have already shown, Jake undergoes an extended identity crisis that calls into question every aspect of his life. As I will subsequently argue, Joshua only thinks that he does. He finds out that the real crisis was not his own but his wife's. His crisis is little more than his recognition of how much he can be blamed for hers.

The large role that Pauline Shapiro plays in the novel that is essentially her husband's story is easily overlooked. Even the title of the book suggests that any polarity of the plot derives not from Pauline's problems as opposed to Joshua's, but from Joshua "then" versus Joshua "now." Joshua, in the present time of the action, thinks so too. He is so intent on returning to Ibiza to undo his ancient fancied failures—the abandonment of a girl with whom he was briefly infatuated and the possible danger he might have brought down on an elderly Jewish couple—that he misses all the signs that could have warned him of his wife's impending collapse. In effect, he does not see the danger in which he left her—the fact that he abandoned her when she most needed him and when she specifically asked him to stay—until it is too late. So the failures that were, he self-indulgently thought, safely contained in his youthful past and waiting to be redeemed, wait for him, instead, in his middle-aged present. That discovery, however, comes late in the novel. Until then the reader, as much as Joshua, is caught up in his first, simple casting of his story.

It is an easy story in which to be caught, for Joshua regularly opposes several intriguing strands from his, to say the least, unusual past against the unfolding drama (a drama admittedly misunderstood) of his present. To start with the more distant past, there are the memories of his early infatuation with his mother, an oedipal situation made more intense by the fact of the father's frequent extended absences. Those absences were professional; the father, after achieving some success as a boxer (the lightweight champion of Canada), had descended to small time racketeering, and a temporary sojourn in the United States often saved him from jail. The father, away, played (one of the comic highlights of the book is the past implicit in Reuben's guarded lectures on sex delivered to an overanxious fifteen-year-old Joshua); the mother resented the child that kept her from the husband with whom she was still much infatuated. Soon she, too, found some solace elsewhere, and young Joshua occasionally found himself locked out of the house. As he remembers, his mother was hardly typical. Even before the advent of the lover she "was utterly unlike the other mothers in the street," in that she was quite "indifferent to his report cards" and totally unconcerned about his prospects of either becoming a doctor or marrying money. Esther Shapiro was not so much interested in her son's prospective career as in her own, and the envisioned career was as idiosyncratic, for a young Jewish mother, as was the object of her ambitions. She planned to become a fan dancer. Another of the comic highlights in the book comes with Joshua's memory of how his mother promised her son a memorable bar-mitzvah party and proceeded to make good by treating the boys who attended to one of her more revealing dances:

"Now I want everybody who got a hard-on watching my act to be a good boy and put up his hand."

Seymour's hand shot up.

"Oh, come on, boys, I couldn't have been that lousy."

Three more hands were raised, then two more.

"Joshua doesn't count, because I'm his mother and it wouldn't be according to Hoyle."

The father is not exactly according to Hoyle either. A sometime rumrunner, a possible bank robber, a torcher, a "bill collector" for a local mobster, Reuben Shapiro still very much loved his son and was determined that Joshua should

have some of the advantages that the father had
lacked, such as a religious education. Reuben,
however, once had to break the fingers of a den-
tist who did not want to pay his gambling debts,
and so the father, most reluctant to meet that
pillar of the local Jewish community at the syn-
agogue, found it necessary to attend to his son's
moral education himself. The discussions on sex
(the guidance that Joshua wants to receive) were
interspersed with lectures on religion and read-
ings from the Bible (the guidance that Reuben
wished to provide). And again the comic possibilities are fully realized as Richler has Reuben
explain, not always inappropriately, Biblical passages in his own inimitable idiom. "The Hebes,"
during their Egyptian captivity, for example,
"were not yet into the needle trade or scrap or
bootlegging or prizefighting or whatever. They
were mostly in construction. Bricks. They were
working like niggers and they were not being
paid a dime." Or "the Book of Job is more than
just another gambling story with a happy ending. It has a moral. These are the Days of Awe,
remember, and I want you to know that if you
continue to believe in God, even when you're up
shit's creek, it can pay off double at the window."
Even the New Testament has a definite place in
Joshua's Jewish education:

> "When you get out into the world and meet
> Christians, you'll find like, they lean on it an awful lot.
> Like, if a guy is ever going to shit on you he usually
> leads with a quote from it. . . . Or, for instance, you're
> running a book and the mayor's bagman wants you to

show your appreciation that he doesn't shut you down. He says, 'Render therefore unto Caesar the things which are Caesar's.' The dirtier the sin, the sweeter the saying. The New Testament covers everything."

Reuben Shapiro is one of Richler's best-conceived characters and is surely the author's most successful comic creation. With his Biblical commentary and with other such observations as, "Shakespeare, . . . Take away the fancy costumes and the swordplay and what are you left with? Poetry, for Christ's sake!" Reuben regularly voices the kind of twisted home truth that has been, since Shakespeare, the hallmark of the wise fool. But there is more to Reuben than his comic contributions to the novel. The main burden of Joshua's earliest memories is his review of the processes whereby, from early childhood to late adolescence, he slowly shifted his allegiances and dramatically revalued both his parents. He comes to see his mother as the impossibly "loopy" character that she always was. And her subsequent career, from artistic dancing to acting in porno films to managing in Manitoba a massage parlor, "Oral Is Beautiful," certainly proves the validity of his reevaluation. He comes to see the core of morality and basic decency that his father, despite his past as a middling boxer and minor racketeer, never lost.

It is at this point also that the reader can begin to see more clearly how the comic excesses of both of the parents are integrated into the more serious business of the plot. Joshua is positive that he has taken the measure of the different members of his family and knows where he and they all stand in relationship to one another; he is also positive that his wife, facing essentially the same task of evaluating her own family, should manage it as expeditiously as he did. After all, how could her immediate relatives—WASPs all—be any more problematic than his own. Besides, when her younger brother resurfaces in Pauline's life, it is perfectly clear to Joshua that Kevin Hornby is a failure and a fraud. If it is obvious to him, surely it is equally obvious to her. Not until her dramatic fall into a nervous breakdown does he perceive that, although his past judgment may have been valid, his present ability to judge has been totally skewed. Pauline does not know where she stands in relationship to Kevin, particularly when the brother's final fiasco leads to a suicide that he clearly suggests Pauline could have prevented. She does not know what the real relationship between her and Joshua is either, and, more to the point, neither does Joshua. Certain that all old uncertainties (except his failure in Spain) have been resolved, he has fitted her into his image of what he would have her be, just as much as he earlier almost wilfully misperceived both his mother and his father.

Pauline's real fall, her succumbing to mental illness, is closely connected in theme and plot with Joshua's earlier fancied fall, his supposed disgrace in Spain. It is therefore appropriate to look at Joshua's one other main memory of times past, his recollections of Ibiza, before returning to the present time of the novel, the failure with Pauline and the other more comic tribulations that also at last catch up with Joshua. Briefly, the Ibiza setback centered, as has already been suggested, on Dr. Dr. Mueller. Joshua, young, naive, intensely Jewish, found that his island idyll was very much disturbed by the arrival of the older German. The issue of Joshua's conflict with this self-proclaimed ex-Nazi was clear before the occasion for it arose. "Are you a man or a mouse?" Dr. Dr. Mueller regularly asked, inviting the younger man to dice for drinks (with dice that were probably loaded, judging from the fact that the Dr. Dr. always won and that most of his public persona was pose). So when Joshua maneuvered into his bed a visiting French girl that Mueller also fancied (and a young lady, it might be added, who required singularly little maneuvering), that triumph clearly proved his manhood at the expense of his hated rival. He was so intent on enjoying the victory—and the spoils—that he never noted how he himself was being maneuvered into a mess.

Thanks to Mueller's telescopic photos of the young lovers disporting themselves, Joshua ran afoul of the law. His efforts to solve that problem only exacerbated it. He secretly visted Mueller's isolated quarters and broke in, to seize the evidence that might be used against him and to find proof, too, of his enemy's Nazi past. The other thereupon claimed that he had been robbed. A break-in had clearly occurred; Joshua, the prime suspect, was given forty-eight hours to leave the island. He had to abandon Monique as well as the Freibergs, an older Jewish couple who were at the time being threatened that their small hotel would be closed down—another consequence, Joshua was sure, of Mueller's evil plotting. Shamed that he could do nothing, he fled. The hasty retreat proved the man a mouse. The proof retrospectively rankles, so much so that Joshua long afterwards still cannot fully believe that his family can love such a failure as himself—thus his eventual determination that he must return to Spain again, to Ibiza even. He will confront Mueller, set right his past defeat, reclaim his long lost manhood. It is, as his wife well knows, a "fool's errand," and, very much a fool, he chooses to run it at a time when he is most needed at home.

"You should have stayed home during her hour of need. Instead you took off for bloody Ibiza, proving yourself an idiot twice." The second proof is the image and the inverse of the first. In both cases, flight demonstrates failure. In both cases, the man he thought he was is not adequate to the test he misperceived. His return to the site of the first test soon reveals to the older Joshua how much the younger Joshua overlooked. The Freibergs were not being persecuted for being Jewish; as hotel owners they were simply being hit for a little standard graft on the trumped-up but never prosecuted charge of faulty wiring. Mariano, the police officer who was so offended by the photos of young Joshua in action, is now into *Hustler* and would like his "old friend," whose earlier exploits he fondly recalls Joshua to send him an occasional issue.

Dr. Dr. Mueller, addicted to foolish claims and disguises, was also Gus McCabe, a writer of German westerns who regularly worked himself up to composition by playing the part of the characters he was about to portray—thus the horse and the odd costumes (the cowboy suit, the Indian outfit, the saloon girl's dress) that Joshua discovered during his break-in. The man merited, Joshua finally realizes, no more than laughter. Already dead, he no longer merits even that. The return to the site of his first test also soon reveals to the older Joshua how much the older Joshua has missed. Richler's careful plotting is here particularly obvious. Joshua sees that the first test was not at all real, and it is precisely then that he discovers the real second test.

He is given one brief intimation of his perilous present before it overwhelms him. "Overcome with both relief and disappointment," he reviews the fiascoes of "ancient history" before embarking on his return home. *"Everybody's lying but you,* Mariano [had] said," when Joshua denied stealing eighteen hundred dollars from Mueller. The memory strikes a chord. "Everybody's a liar but you, Joshua said" when Kevin insisted that he was not guilty of the stock market swindles of which he is accused. Of course the two are not brothers-in-innocence beneath their strained brother-in-law relationship. It is, Joshua reassures himself, "absolutely impossible" that "Kevin was telling the truth." Nonetheless, kinship must be acknowledged. Kevin "was Pauline's brother. The senator's only

son. He would have to be helped." Joshua,
"exhilarated" by his new resolve and ready to let
the past—"another time, another place"—at last
rest, finally manages to get a telephone call
through to Pauline to tell her of his immediate
return and of the dawning new order. At which
point time past and time present, Ibiza and
Montreal, come crashing together. Kevin has
just committed suicide; Pauline is tottering
toward her mental and emotional collapse;
Joshua at last sees where his test and his failure had loomed all along. His return to Spain
has only completed an ironic circle. Joshua
"now" continues also to be Joshua "then."
Joshua "then" foreshadows what Joshua "now"
becomes.

The thematic connections between the
problems faced by the husband and the wife are
important, but they are not obvious, for these
parallels are worked into characters who, at first,
do not seem to play a large role in the action. Yet
the apparent insignificance of Pauline's mother,
for example, is mostly an accident of perspective
and a consequence of the fact that Joshua tells
the story. Since Joshua is an obviously limited
narrator, the reader must sometimes look beyond the story as he tells it. So Joshua at one
point briefly notes the essential facts of his
mother-in-law's life, but the reader can observe—as Joshua does not—how suggestively
those details resemble, in magnified form, the
essential facts of Joshua's mother's life. When
Mrs. Hornby decides that her husband does not
measure up, she leaves him to live among the

gigolos, occasionaly dragging her children in her wake. Joshua, as a child, was sometimes locked out of the house while his mother entertained a male guest; Pauline and her bother, as small children, were merely shut up in the next room—well within range of the sound of their mother loud at love. In essence, this mother did her own thing in a crudely selfish fashion that Esther Shapiro, also dubiously intent on being her own woman, does not remotely approximate.

Neither are the two fathers, Senator Hornby and ex-con Shapiro, as dissimilar as their different stations in life might suggest. For that matter, their stations are not actually that different. Senator Hornby occupies a low position on the highest level—not quite the man he should have been, a senator and not a cabinet minister. Reuben is similarly situationed several rungs below the senator—also not quite (socially speaking) the man he should have been. The two older men are also, throughout the novel, fast friends, and both are concerned with the happiness of Joshua and Pauline. Indeed, Joshua, for all practical purposes, becomes Senator Hornby's son, the son that Kevin fails to be, and Pauline is, for Reuben, much more a daughter than a daughter-in-law. Nevertheless, although each father was a decent man, each was also caught in an unhappy marriage and saw the unhappiness in which he participated touch others besides himself. Here too, considering Pauline's account of how her younger brother was "destroyed" when he became "a counter in my parents' quarrel," and not discounting Kevin's considerable talents for destroying himself, it is obvious that the problems in Pauline's family far outweighed those in Joshua's. Her relationship with her father, whom she does love, remains deeply ambivalent. Joshua, as an adult, has no difficulty coming to terms with his father. His love for Reuben is simple and direct.

Pauline's family problems apparently began with the collapsing marriage of her parents, but they soon centered on another family member. The young daughter saw her beautiful younger brother idolized at school, criticized and cut down at home. She sympathized with the subterfuges whereby he tried to claim status in his father's eyes, while also being party to and profiting from his mother's lax morality. Pauline also continued to judge Kevin as a victim of circumstance long after the preponderance of evidence well might have pointed to quite another conclusion. But even Pauline finally gave up on Kevin. So, in the "now" of her middle-aged life, she is surprised when he returns from what had seemed a permanent exile in Bermuda, surprised when he is taken in by a wealthy patron as the ostensible manager of an investment venture, but not at all surprised when it becomes clear that the business has been ineptly and probably illegally managed. Her ostensible crisis is the consequence of Kevin's failure as well as Joshua's. Kevin requests a lie that might keep him from jail, while Joshua makes it clear that he would be appalled to have his wife party to a cover-up.

Yet the issues here run much deeper, and there is still a parallel between Pauline's difficulties with Kevin and the early trials and tribulations of a Joshua—who had no siblings—in love. Richler both raises and skirts—successfully, I think—an issue melodramatic enough that, mishandled, it could easily undo the novel. At several points there are hints of some kind of past incestuous relationship, perhaps actual incest, perhaps sublimated, between brother and sister. Those hints remain simply that; the question is never resolved one way or the other. Yet they serve several clear purposes. Joshua, for example, is, from the start, subject to dark suspicions. His immediate reaction to the brother-in-law he had not previously met is to treat that relative as a rival for Pauline's favors. Pauline would be choosing the rival if she lied to save him—thus the covert pressure that she should not do so, which is one reason why she subsequently pays so painfully for Kevin's suicide. But the crucial parallel is only once suggested in the novel. "Darling, I don't know how many times we've compared childhoods over the years," Joshua observes to Pauline soon after Kevin enters on the scene. "I haven't held anything back. Not even Ed Ryan. But there's always been a bit of a gap on your end." The "bit of a gap," Pauline at once acknowledges, is Kevin. More significant than the gap, however, is the way in which it is noted. How lucky for Joshua that "everything" is epitomized by Ed Ryan—not some fiasco of his own, but his mother's sad affair. And why not tell most of the story of

Monique? For all Joshua's personal suspicions of private failure, the public details will still flatter him. In short, his past sexual misadventures are minor affairs and cherished memories compared even to what he knows of Pauline's promiscuous London ventures. Yet her public past may be small potatoes too, compared to her possible private one. The point is that, in a story in which Joshua laments that he "did not know," Richler suggests that there is perhaps much more that his protagonist might never know. Thus perspective itself, the fact that it is and must be only Joshua's story, is put in perspective. Were the narration Pauline's, she well might laugh for the little things that made him sad.

The novel, with Kevin and Pauline, suicide and possible incest, verges on some of the darker business of Revenge Tragedy. Richler counters such tendencies with a large dose of what one reviewer has aptly termed "Revenge Comedy."[5] Joshua does not take time to assess carefully Pauline's current crisis partly because he is caught in his own past and partly because he is also particularly concerned with the present lives of present and former friends. He remains true, in his fashion, to his own origins by punishing those who have betrayed a shared St. Urbain Street upbringing by becoming rich and uppity:

> "Joshua, what are you doing here?"
> "I come up here for the fresh air, Irving. You have no idea how it stinks down below. We even have niggers on our street."
> "You're supposed to say 'blacks' now. How would you like to be called a kike?"
> "I'm a Jew, Irving, you're a kike."

This same character, Irving Pinsky, prides himself on his wine cellar. He shows it to Joshua once and lets that old acquaintance "fondle" some of the more expensive bottles. The cellar is subsequently broken into, all the labels removed, and the bottles rearranged. Since nothing was taken, the insurance will not pay. Pinsky is most put out as he tells this tale of woe to a commiserating Joshua:

> "Fortunately, a man with your educated palate could open any one of these bottles and tell not only the vineyard, but the vintage."
> "Certainly. But how would I know which one to open?"
> "Red with meat. White for fish."
> "I wish I had your simple tastes."

There are numerous such episodes running through the novel, all of which help to give *Joshua Then and Now* a pervasive tone of comic social criticism. That same tone is fostered by Joshua's frequent sardonic observations on the world around him. Note, for example, his description of the consequences that followed the surprising election of the Parti Québécois and the sudden prospects of an independent Quebec: "Almost everybody he knew was jittery, drinking more, inclined to stumble out of bed at 3 a.m. to jot down a list of redeemable assets on the back of an envelope. Or study French verbs." It should also be noted that Richler does not exempt Joshua from satirical judgments similar to those that Joshua readily dispenses. Of course the satire in both cases is rather gentle. When, for example, he finds that an old acquaintance,

Yossel Kugelman, is now—as "Dr. Jonathan Cole,
author of *My Kind, Your Kind, Mankind,"*—
one of Pauline's physicians, Joshua soon recol-
lects the checkered past of Mrs. Cole and his own
youthful "innings" with her on her parents' sofa.
But the Coles remember too:

"I remember your father's picture on the front page
of the *Herald*—wearing handcuffs. I was at your bar-
mitzvah, and I still remember what happened there.
We know you and what you come from. And I've got
news for you. Bessie told me about her *one* date with
the great Mr. Shapiro. Pretending to be a McGill
student. Calling yourself Robert Jordan. She thought
you were pathetic, that's what."
    Remembering, Joshua blushed.
    "She dines out on that one to this day," Yossel
continued.

The novel shows balanced comedy, but the
comedy itself is still more subtly balanced with
other elements in the novel. What Robert Harlow has termed "Comic Revenge," for example,
finally devolves toward tragic farce. Joshua, almost apprehended at the scene of his final puni-
tive break-in, tries to make a clear getaway and is
almost killed in the resultant automobile accident. The novel begins with the consequence of
this late action, as well as with the consequences
of a few other actions that are also only slowly
revealed. When we first encounter Joshua, he is
beginning to recover from a close encounter
with death (a serious effect of a comic cause),
and he has also been most publicly but quite
mistakenly labeled a homosexual (a comic effect
of a comic cause). A fake correspondence of

scurrilously slanderous homosexual love letters once concocted in London as a possibly saleable item by (and between) Joshua and another impecunious young writer is finally sold. The seller is the son of the London writer whose wife was for a time Joshua's mistress. So Joshua, as he later realizes when many wheels begin to come full circle, was this angry young Englishman's Ed Ryan. The letters were sold to Pauline's first husband, now the curator of the rare manuscript collection at a wealthy western Canadian university. He, too, has old scores to settle. Naturally the more juicy items in the collection are made public. All of which serves—since the car accident during the chase and the surfacing of the old fake letters both occur after Joshua's return from Spain and Pauline's breakdown—to pile a mock physical crisis (of course Joshua will survive his injuries) and a mock sexual crisis (of course Joshua is not a homosexual) on top of the serious and real crisis, the failure with Pauline, which itself quite superceded the old false crisis of the supposed failure in Ibiza. It is a difficult sandwich to sort out, and one of the pleasures in reading the novel is to savor how carefully Richler puts it all together. That care extends up to the very end. Pauline's final return is justified by the numerous reversals and switches that have taken place in the novel, such as Joshua entering the hospital soon after she leaves it. The final scene of the two meeting in the garden is not the "soft-centered, unearned tableau of marital felicity among the growing vegetables" that one critic has suggested.[6] Quite the contrary; the novel ends with what can best be described as a mock remarriage of two middle-aged and far-from-perfect lovers in a far-from-flourishing garden—an ironic twist to the traditional comic concluson, the requisite marriage, and thus a most appropriate ending for a comic/ironic work.

The ex-expatriate author back in Canada sends his ex-expatriate protagonist wandering once more. More specifically, Richler sends Joshua to Spain, which, by calling to mind André Bennett, another Canadian protagonist in Spain, gives us also a version of Richler then and now. *The Acrobats* showed us the young author trying too hard and demonstrating mostly that he had not yet mastered his medium. *Joshua Then and Now* shows us the mature writer at the top of his talent and in total control of his technique. It is a finished comic work, carefully structured and thematically subtle, whereas *The Acrobats* was not artistically finished in any sense. Taken together, the two novels show that, in contradistinction to his most recent protagonist, Richler now is not the same as Richler then. On that note I will conclude this study. Which is another way of saying that the author is to be particularly praised for his progression, for the extent and the rapidity of his development, for the degree to which growth has been sustained. After the two "first novels" comes the surprisingly complex *A Choice of Enemies*, a book considerably better than its plotting might suggest. Then four of the next five novels are, in their different ways, major works. And even *The Incomparable Atuk* has its own appealing aura of very successful sophomore comedy. But it is *The Apprenticeship of Duddy Kravitz, Cocksure, St. Urbain's Horseman*, and, finally, *Joshua Then and Now* that particularly prove Richler's success as a novelist and demonstrate that the young writer who left Canada to compete on the larger stage of the western world has become, as he intended, a significant voice in contemporary literature.

Notes

1. *THE STREET* AND BEYOND: STARTING OUT IN THE MONTREAL GHETTO

1. In some details the protagonist of *The Street* clearly is not Mordecai Richler. The former has, for example, an older sister; the latter has an older brother. Rifka, the older sister in *The Street*, is also, it might be noted, present under the same name as Jacob Hersh's older sister in *St. Urbain's Horseman.*

2. Judy Margolis, "Mom of a Smaller Hero," A Review of *The Errand Runner: Reflections of a Rabbi's Daughter*, by Leah Rosenberg, John Wiley & Sons, in *Books in Canada*, March 1981, pp. 15–16.

3. Sandra Martin, "Insult and Injury," *Books in Canada*, March 1981, p. 5.

4. Graeme Gibson, *Eleven Canadian Novelists Interviewed by Graeme Gibson* (Toronto: Anansi, 1973), p. 271.

5. Nathan Cohen, "A Conversation with Mordecai Richler," *The Tamarack Review*, no. 2 (Winter 1957), p. 20.

6. Ibid., p. 7.

7. George Woodcock, untitled entry on Mordecai Richler in *Contemporary Novelists*, ed. James Vinson (London: St. James Press, 1976), p. 1169.

8.   Tom Marshall, "Third Solitude: Canadian as Jew," in *The Canadian Novel: Here and Now*, vol. 1, ed. John Moss (Toronto: N C Press, 1978), p. 150.

9.   Robert Harlow, "Telling it in Garth," A Review of *Joshua Then and Now* by Mordecai Richler, in *Books in Canada*, May 1980, p. 7.

10. "Foreword" to *Hunting Tigers Under Glass* (1968; rpt. London: Panther Books, 1971), p. 9.

11. Donald Cameron, "Mordecai Richler: The Reticent Moralist," in *Conversations with Canadian Novelists*, Part Two (Toronto: Macmillan, 1973), p. 117.

12. Ibid., p. 117.

13. Ibid., p. 9.

14. Ibid., p. 8.

15. Ibid., p. 8.

16. Gibson, p. 280.

17. From "A Sense of the Ridiculous: Paris, 1951 and After." In this essay, originally published in *New American Review*, no. 4 (Aug. 1968), pp. 114–34 and reprinted in *Shovelling Trouble, Notes on an Endangered Species and Others*, and *The Great Comic Book Heroes and Other Essays*, Richler gives an extended account of his two years in Paris.

18. Cohen, p. 13.

19. *Times Literary Supplement*, 29 (July 1955): 425. Quoted in Michael Darling, "Mordecai Richler: An Annotated Bibliography," in *The Annotated Bibliography of Canada's Major Authors*, vol. 1, ed. Robert Lecker and Jack David (Downsview, Ont.: ECW Press, 1979), p. 194.

20. Richler, it should be noted, judges the by-now-standard ploy of the writer teaching university courses on creative writing to be a selling out. He

has twice been briefly a writer-in-residence and found it a "crushing business" (Martin, p. 3).

21. Cameron, p. 125.
22. Ibid., p. 118.
23. Ibid., p. 119.
24. John Metcalf, "Black Humour: An Interview with Mordecai Richler," *Journal of Canadian Fiction*, 3, no. 1 (Winter 1974), p. 73.
25. Quoted in "Mordecai Richler" entry in *Contemporary Authors: A Bio-Bibliographical Guide*, vol. 65–68, ed. Jane A. Bowden (Detroit: Gale Research, 1977), p. 491.
26. Cameron, p. 123.
27. *Shovelling Trouble*, (Toronto: McClelland and Stewart, 1972), pp. 18–19.

2.   *THE ACROBATS*: A FIRST TRY
AT ARTISTIC BALANCE

1. George Bowering, "And the Sun Goes Down: Richler's First Novel," *Canadian Literature*, no. 29 (Summer 1966), p. 11.
2. This same point is made in slightly different terms by George Woodcock in *Mordecai Richler*, Canadian Writers, no. 6 (Toronto: McClelland and Stewart, 1971), p. 16.
3. Ibid., *Mordecai Richler*, p. 13.
4. Ibid., *Mordecai Richler*, p. 17.
5. Ibid., *Mordecai Richler*, p. 17.
6. This extended compassion is important to Richler. As he has observed, "running through all my novels, I think, there has been a persistent attempt to make a case for the ostensibly unsympathetic man" (Cameron, p. 117).

3. *SON OF A SMALLER HERO*:
THE PROTAGONIST
CLAIMS HIS MAJORITY

1. George Woodcock, *Mordecai Richler*, Canadian Writers, no. 6 (Toronto: McClelland and Stewart, 1971), p. 27.
2. This same "goy" is reintroduced into the plot later in the novel and clearly shown to be a conniver and a cheat.
3. Although the matter is not conclusively resolved in the novel, the mother probably does die soon after Noah leaves.

4. POLITICS, LOVE, AND LOSS:
A CHOICE OF ENEMIES

1. This point is made by another critic who observed: "Having succeeded in writing two first novels, Mordecai Richler was too astute to risk a third." Peter Scott, "A Choice of Certainties," *The Tamarack Review*, no. 8 (Summer 1958), p. 75.
2. Pierre Cloutier, "Mordecai Richler's Exiles: *A Choice of Enemies*," *Journal of Canadian Fiction*, 1, no. 2 (Spring 1972), p. 43.
3. Ibid., p. 45.
4. Ibid., p. 45.
5. In this respect he is, as Cloutier notes, "pure Hemingway, an individual traumatized by the random, irrational" nature of war (p. 45).
6. Scott, p. 81. Much more convincingly Kerry McSweeney, in "Revaluing Mordecai Richler," *Studies in Canadian Literature* 4, no. 2 (1979), p. 124, observes that we finally see "a worn out,

morally numbed man passively sinking into a marital limbo with a shallow, opportunistic and ugly wife."

5. THE ADVENTURES OF A "PUSHERKE" IN *THE APPRENTICESHIP OF DUDDY* KRAVITZ

1. A. R. Bevan, "Introduction" to *The Apprenticeship of Duddy Kravitz*, New Canadian Library, no. 66 (Toronto: McClelland and Stewart, 1969), n.p. For Warren Tallman's assessments of the novel, see "Richler and the Faithless City," *Canadian Literature*, no. 3 (Winter 1960), pp. 62–64 and "Wolf in the Snow. Part Two: The House Repossessed," *Canadian Literature*, no. 6 (Autumn 1960), pp. 41–48.

2. George Woodcock, *Mordecai Richler*, Canadian Writers, no. 6 (Toronto: McClelland and Stewart, 1971), p. 39.

3. "I'm afraid I've never written very well about women. I think my feminine characters tend to be one-dimensional," Richler observed in his interview with Graeme Gibson, *Eleven Canadian Novelists Interviewed by Graeme Gibson* (Toronto: Anansi, 1973), p. 287.

4. John Ferns, "Sympathy and Judgement in Mordecai Richler's *The Apprenticeship of Duddy Kravitz,*" *Journal of Canadian Fiction* 3, no. 1 (Winter 1974), p. 80.

5. D. J. Dooley, *Moral Vision in the Canadian Novel* (Toronto: Clarke, Irwin, 1979), p. 98.

6. David Myers, "Mordecai Richler as Satirist," *ARIEL: A Review of International English Literature*, 4, no. 1 (1973), pp. 51–52.

7. Richler has suggested that the reader's final

reaction to Duddy should be the recogniton, "well, yes, this is another human being" (Gibson, p. 292).

6.   *THE INCOMPARABLE ATUK*: A CANADIAN ESKIMO'S AMERICAN DREAM

1.   Richler's critics have generally ignored or passed quickly over *The Incomparable Atuk*. George Woodcock, for example, in his book *Mordecai Richler*, Canadian Writers no. 6 (Toronto; McClelland and Stewart, 1971), devotes only three pages to this novel, which he characterizes as an "entertainment and little more" (p. 44).

2.   *George Woodcock, Mordecai Richler,*

3.   Woodcock, *Mordecai Richler*, p. 45.

4.   Woodcock, *Mordecai Richler*, p. 46.

7.   POPULAR CULTURE, BLACK COMEDY, AND *COCKSURE*

1.   "On one level the two things that have satisfied me most are *The Apprenticeship of Duddy Kravitz* and *Cocksure,"* Richler has observed in one of his interviews. Graeme Gibson, *Eleven Canadian Novelists Interviewed by Graeme Gibson* (Toronto: Anansi, 1973), p. 275.

2.   This point is well made by Woodcock, who observes that numerous "features of *Cocksure* belong to the world of sexual fantasy and bawdy jokes that beguiles adolescent boys." George Woodcock, *Mordecai Richler*, Canadian Writers, no. 6 (Toronto: MvClelland and Stewart, 1971), p. 50.

3.   Ibid., pp. 53–54.

8. *ST. URBAIN'S HORSEMAN:*
THE PROTAGONIST ON TRIAL

1. Zailig Pollock, "The Trial of Jake Hersh," *Journal of Canadian Fiction*, no. 22 (1978), p. 93.
2. John Moss, "Richler's Horseman," in *The Canadian Novel: Here and Now*, vol. 1, ed. John Moss (Toronto: NC press, 1978), pp. 156–157.
3. Nancy is one of the few exceptions to Richler's self-confessed inability to portray convincing women. See chapter 5, note 3.
4. Wilfred Cude, "The Golem as Metaphor for Art: The Monster Takes Meaning in *St. Urbain's Horseman*," *Journal of Canadian Studies*, 12, no. 2 (Spring 1977), p. 55.
5. G. David Sheps, "Waiting for Joey: The Theme of the Vicarious in *St. Urbain's Horseman*," *Journal of Canadian Fiction* 3, no. 1 (Winter 1974), p. 84.
6. Ibid., p. 84.
7. Ibid., p. 84.
8. This point is made by Pollock, p. 100.
9. Moss, p. 157.
10. Cude, p. 54.
11. The connection is effectively drawn by Pollock, p. 103.
12. Sheps also points out how "timid" and "vicarious" Jake's revenge is (p. 91).
13. Richler, talking of this novel, emphasizes: "It's *meant* to be elusive and complex, it's *meant* to be ambivalent, full of ambiguities.... Every ambiguity is intentionally there, and I think that is part of the novel's strength myself." Donald Cameron, "Mordecai Richler: The Reticent Moralist," in *Conversations with Canadian Novelists*, Part Two (Toronto: Macmillan, 1973), p. 124.
14. Cude, p. 68

9. *JOSHUA THEN AND NOW,*
OR *THE TRIAL REVISITED*

1. George Woodcock, "The Wheel of Exile," *The Tamarack Review,* no. 58 (1971), p. 65.
2. Woodcock, "The Wheel of Exile," pp. 65, 72.
3. Kerry McSweeney, "Richler's Fireworks," *Essays on Canadian Writing,* no. 20 (Winter 1980–81), p. 161.
4. Ibid., p. 161.
5. Robert Harlow, "Telling it in Garth," A Review of *Joshua Then and Now* by Mordecai Richler, in *Books in Canada,* May 1980, p. 7.
6. McSweeney, p. 163.

Bibliography

BOOKS BY MORDECAI RICHLER

The Acrobats. London: André Deutsch, 1954; New York: G.P. Putnam's Sons, 1954.

Son of a Smaller Hero. London: André Deutsch, 1955.

A Choice of Enemies. London: André Deutsch, 1957.

The Apprenticeship of Duddy Kravitz. London: André Deutsch, 1959; Boston: Little, Brown, 1959.

The Incomparable Atuk. London: André Deutsch, 1963; Toronto: McClelland and Stewart, 1963.

Cocksure. London: Weidenfeld and Nicolson, 1968; New York: Simon and Schuster, 1968; Toronto: McClelland and Stewart, 1968.

Hunting Tigers Under Glass: Essays and Reports. Toronto: McClelland and Stewart, 1968.

The Street. Toronto: McClelland and Stewart, 1969.

St. Urbain's Horseman. London: Weidenfeld and Nicolson, 1971; New York: Alfred A. Knopf, 1971; Toronto: McClelland and Stewart, 1971.

Shovelling Trouble. Toronto: McClelland and Stewart, 1972.

Notes on an Endangered Species and Others. New York: Alfred A. Knopf, 1974.

Jacob Two-Two Meets the Hooded Fang. Toronto: McClelland and Stewart, 1975.

Images of Spain. Text by Mordecai Richler, photography by Peter Christopher. Toronto: McClelland and Stewart, 1977; New York: Norton, 1977.

195

The Great Comic Book Heroes and Other Essays. New
      Canada Library, no. 152. Toronto: McClelland
      and Stewart, 1978.
Joshua Then and Now. Toronto: McClelland and
      Stewart, 1980; New York: Alfred A. Knopf, 1980.

BIBLIOGRAPHIC REFERENCE

Darling, Michael. "Mordecai Richler: An Annotated
      Bibliography." In *The Annotated Bibliography of
      Canada's Major Authors,* vol. 1, edited by Robert
      Lecker and Jack David. Downsview, Ontario:
      ECW Press, 1979. (Considerations of space pre-
      clude listing Richler's voluminous occasional
      writing. Readers interested in his journalism,
      book reviews, and other shorter works are
      referred to this bibliography.)

SELECTED CRITICISM

Bevan, A. R. Introduction to *The Apprenticeship of
      Duddy Kravitz.* New Canada Library, no. 66. To-
      ronto: McClelland and Stewart, 1969.
Birbalsingh, F. M. "Mordecai Richler and the Jewish-
      Canadian Novel." *Journal of Commonwealth Lit-
      erature* 7 (1972), 72–82.
Bowering, George. "And the Sun Goes Down:
      Richler's First Novel." *Canadian Literature,* no. 29
      (1966), 7–17.
Cloutier, Pierre. "Mordecai Richler's Exiles: *A Choice
      of Enemies." Journal of Canadian Fiction* 1, no. 2
      (1972), 43–49.
Cohen, Nathan. "Heroes of the Richler View." *The
      Tamarack Review,* no. 6 (1958), 47–60.

Cohn-Sfetcu, Ofelia. "Of Self, Temporal Cubism, and Metaphor: Mordecai Richler's *St. Urbain's Horseman.*" *International Fiction Review* 3, no. 1 (1976), 30–34.

Cude, Wilfred. "The Golem as Metaphor for Art: The Monster Takes Meaning in *St. Urbain's Horseman.*" *Journal of Canadian Fiction* 12, no. 2 (1977), 50–69.

Dooley, D. J. "Mordecai Richler and Duddy Kravitz: A Moral Apprenticeship?" (Ch. 8). In his *Moral Vision in the Canadian Novel.* Toronto: Clarke, Irwin, 1979.

Ferns, John. "Sympathy and Judgement in Mordecai Richler's *The Apprenticeship of Duddy Kravitz.*" *Journal of Canadian Fiction* 3, no. 1 (1974), 77–82.

Greenstein, Michael. "The Apprenticeship of Noah Adler." *Canadian Literature*, no. 78 (1978), 43–51.

Kattan, Naïm. "Mordecai Richler: Craftsman or Artist." *Canadian Literature*, no. 21 (1964), 46–51.

Marshall, Tom. "Third Solitude: Canadian as Jew." In *The Canadian Novel Here and Now*, vol. 1, edited by John Moss. Toronto: NC Press, 1978.

Martin, Sandra. "Insult and Injury." *Books in Canada*, March 1981, pp. 3–7.

McGregor, Grant. "Duddy Kravitz: From Apprentice to Legend." *Journal of Canadian Fiction*, no. 30 (1980), 132–140.

McSweeney, Kerry. "Revaluing Mordecai Richler." *Studies in Canadian Literature* 4, no. 2 (1979), 120–131.

———. "Richler's Fireworks." *Essays on Canadian Writing*, no. 20 (Winter 1980–81), 160–164.

Moss, John. *Patterns of Isolation in English Canadian Fiction.* Toronto: McClelland and Stewart, 1974.

———. "Richler's Horseman." In *The Canadian Novel Here and Now*, vol. 1, ed. by John Moss. Toronto: NC Press, 1978.

Myers, David. "Mordecai Richler as Satirist." *Ariel* 4, no. 1 (1973), 47–61.

New, William H. "The Apprenticeship of Discovery: Richler and MacLennan." *Canadian Literature*, no. 29 (1966), 108–127.

Northey, Margot. "Satiric Grotesque: *Cocksure*" (Ch. 12). In her *The Haunted Wilderness: The Gothic and Grotesque in Canadian Fiction*. Toronto: University of Toronto Press, 1976.

Ower, John, "Sociology, Psychology, and Satire in *The Apprenticeship of Duddy Kravitz*." *Modern Fiction Studies*, 22 (1976), 413–428.

Pollock, Zailig. "The Trial of Jake Hersh." *Journal of Canadian Fiction*, no. 22 (1978), 93–105.

Scott, Peter. "A Choice of Certainties." *The Tamarack Review*, no. 8 (1958), 73–82.

Sheps, G. David, ed. *Mordecai Richler*. Critical Views on Canadian Writers, no. 6. Toronto: McGraw-Hill Ryerson, 1971.

———. "Waiting for Joey: The Theme of the Vicarious in *St. Urbain's Horseman*." *Journal of Canadian Fiction* 3, no. 1 (1974), 83–92.

Tallman, Warren. "Richler and the Faithless City." *Canadian Literature*, no. 3 (1960), 62–64.

———. "Wolf in the Snow. Part Two: The House Repossessed." *Canadian Literature*, no. 6 (1960), 41–48.

———. "Need for Laughter." *Canadian Literature*, no. 56 (1973), 71–83.

Warkentin, Germaine. "*Cocksure:* An Abandoned Introduction." *Journal of Canadian Fiction* 4, no. 3 (1975), 81–86.

Woodcock, George. *Mordecai Richler*. Canadian Writers, no. 6. Toronto: McClelland and Stewart, 1971.

———. "The Wheel of Exile." *The Tamarack Review*, no. 58 (1971), 65–72.

Index

LITERATURE AND LIFE SERIES
(Formerly Modern Literature and World Dramatists)
GENERAL EDITOR: PHILIP WINSOR

Selected list of titles:

Complete list of titles in the series available from publisher on request.